MANAGING EMPLOYEE PERFORMANCE IN SEVEN STEPS

Kieran Baldwin

Published in 2008 by Kieran Baldwin

ISBN: 978-0-9559836-0-3

Printed and bound by Antony Rowe, Eastbourne, East Sussex

Note: The material contained in this book is set out in good faith for general guidance and no liability can be accepted for loss or expense incurred as a result of relying in particular circumstances on statements made in this book. The law and regulations are complex and liable to change, and readers should check the current position with the relevant authorities before making personal arrangements.

Contents

List of illustrations   **- 6 -**

Preface   **- 7 -**

1. Practising performance management   **- 11 -**
Managing performance is a manager's responsibility   - 11 -
Defining performance management practice   - 11 -
Performance management systems   - 12 -
Developing performance management practice   - 15 -
Case studies   - 16 -
Case studies - Commentary   - 17 -
Points to consider   - 17 -

2. Defining the job – Step one   **- 19 -**
Explaining requirements clearly   - 19 -
Using task checklists   - 20 -
Managing the 'ways' as well as the 'whats'   - 21 -
Demonstrating empathy develops trust   - 23 -
Constructing task statements   - 23 -
Producing task statements   - 25 -
Regularly reviewing step one   - 27 -
Case studies   - 27 -
Case studies - Commentary   - 28 -
Points to consider   - 29 -

3. Providing job related training – Step two   **- 31 -**
Defining job related training   - 31 -
Establishing the importance of job related training   - 31 -
Delivering training   - 32 -
Assessing knowledge and skill levels   - 34 -
Training removes fear   - 35 -
Case studies   - 36 -
Case studies – Commentary   - 38 -
Points to consider   - 38 -

4. Understanding and influencing attitudes – Step three   **- 39 -**
Defining attitude   - 39 -
Developing work related attitudes   - 39 -
Identifying a person's attitudes   - 40 -
Reviewing 'steps one and two'   - 40 -
Understanding how attitudes influence behaviour   - 41 -
Attitude is sometimes 'step one'   - 42 -
Case studies   - 43 -
Case studies - Commentary   - 44 -
Points to consider   - 44 -

5. Creating the right working environment – Step four   **- 45 -**
Analysing the environment   - 45 -
External motivation   - 45 -
Monitoring and control   - 49 -
Exercising self discipline   - 51 -
Case studies   - 53 -
Case studies - Commentary   - 55 -
Points to consider   - 56 -

6. Understanding and managing habit – Step five   **- 57 -**
Defining habit   - 57 -
Defining criticism   - 58 -
Managers managing themselves   - 62 -
Demotivating staff   - 67 -
The vicious circle   - 68 -
Developing genuine self confidence   - 71 -
Case studies   - 72 -
Case studies - Commentary   - 74 -
Points to consider   - 74 -

7. Assessing aptitudes – Step six   **- 76 -**
Defining aptitudes   - 76 -
Assessing aptitude   - 77 -
Accepting the job is unsuitable   - 79 -
Case studies   - 80 -
Case studies - Commentary   - 82 -
Points to consider   - 82 -

8. Identfying internal motivation needs – Step seven   **- 83 -**
Defining internal motivation   - 83 -
Exploring an individual's motivation   - 83 -
Confronting a lack of job motivation   - 84 -
The connection between aptitudes and internal motivation   - 86 -
Case studies   - 87 -
Case studies - Commentary   - 89 -
Points to consider   - 89 -

9. Defining good performance   **- 90 -**
Defining good performance – the options   - 90 -
Option one   - 90 -
Option two   - 93 -
Option three   - 93 -
Assessing the quality of staff and managers   - 94 -
Case studies   - 95 -
Case studies - Commentary   - 96 -
Points to consider   - 96 -

10. Debriefing skills   **- 97 -**
Types of interview   - 97 -
Debriefing interviews   - 97 -
Influencing the debriefee's attitude   - 99 -
Debriefing skills   - 101 -
Summary   - 103 -
Case studies   - 103 -
Case studies - Commentary   - 105 -
Points to consider   - 105 -

11. Implementing changes successfully   **- 107 -**
Initiating change   - 107 -
Responding to change   - 107 -
Introducing change and the 'seven steps'   - 108 -
Controlling the introduction of change   - 113 -
Case studies   - 113 -
Case studies - Commentary   - 114 -
Points to consider   - 115 -

12. **Running staff meetings** **- 116 -**
   The purpose of a staff meeting - 116 -
   Structuring the meeting - 116 -
   Controlling the meeting - 121 -
   Assessing the effectiveness of meetings - 122 -
   Case studies - 123 -
   Case studies - Commentary - 124 -
   Points to consider - 125 -

13. **Performance Management Practice in a business context** **- 126 -**
   Specialist knowledge and skills - 127 -
   Management style - 128 -
   Organisation culture - 131 -
   Influencing how managers operate - 132 -
   Managers conform or leave - 134 -
   Case studies - 136 -
   Case studies - Commentary - 137 -
   Points to consider - 138 -

14. **A Case Study** **- 139 -**
   Introduction - 139 -
   The problem - 139 -
   Gathering information - 140 -
   Reviewing the information - 144 -
   Taking action - 145 -
   Following up - 146 -
   Identifying the cause - 148 -
   Solving the problem - 149 -
   The benefits for the organisation - 150 -
   Conclusion - 150 -

   Glossary **- 152 -**

   Index **- 154 -**

List of illustrations

Figure 1. Uncontrolled reaction to criticism   - 61 -

Figure 2. Controlled reaction to criticism   - 63 -

Figure 3. The manager's vicious circle   - 70 -

Figure 4. The vicious circle template   - 71 -

Figure 5. Performance management practice in context   - 126 -

Figure 6. Equating inputs with outputs   - 135 -

Preface

Who should read this book?

In most businesses promotion involves assuming responsibility for the performance of others. Successful accountants and sales people in large organizations, can often only progress by assuming line management responsibilities. Sole traders who grow their businesses find they have to employ others. Success in any job invariably results in a person having to worry about the performance of others. As a business grows or a career develops, sound technical skills or good inter-personal skills need to be augmented by effective people management skills. This book is about helping people make that transition. It is also about helping those who may be struggling to make that transition. The techniques described will harness the attributes of those naturally inclined to lead others and support those who are less inclined. Naturally gifted leaders, without technique, can often cause as many problems as those who are less gifted. The majority of the most naturally gifted sportsmen and women have only achieved success by improving and maintaining techniques relevant to their sports. People management is no different. If you manage people or you are about to assume that responsibility, this book will help you. It is not just a textbook. It has been written to provide practical guidance over time and be a constant source of reference as problems or fresh challenges are encountered.

Techniques described are practical not theoretical

Many management courses and textbooks tend to concentrate on theory rather than practice. Theory is important but if the manager cannot put the theory into practice, money and time has been wasted. The notion that managers should work out the practical application of theory is fundamentally flawed. In my experience it just does not happen, as daily workloads and crises swamp even the most enthusiastic student.

Training that stops at the stage of explaining theory is doing half the job. I came to this conclusion in the 1970s when as a Training Manager I sent managers on 'good' courses that failed to produce desired results. Thus the seed of the 'seven steps' was sown. Over time I established there were several reasons why training did not always result in changed behaviour in practice. I also found that these reasons could be categorised and addressed in a logical sequence.

The seven steps

The 'seven steps' is a framework that enables the user to concentrate on practical application of theory. I developed the 'seven steps' framework and found it helped me manage performance effectively. The framework also helped my direct reports manage their people and so on down through the management structure. We talked a common language; a vital first step in a hierarchical organisation.

The 'seven steps' framework has been widely used and is still used in highly demanding business environments.

Performance management inevitably involves criticism

Addressing issues inevitably involves the giving and receiving of criticism. An environment in which the giving and receiving criticism is accepted is vital if improvement and development is to occur. This potentially divisive topic is dealt with fully in chapter 6.

Defining words

I discovered very early on in my management career that words like 'motivation' and 'attitude' were used a great deal when managers discussed staff. What also became clear was that there was no common definition of these words. In a group of, say, six managers one could find six different definitions. How can we hope to communicate if we do not share a common definition of words used?

As I use various 'management' words or phrases I will define them. The definitions will not always be pure text book definitions, but then in my experience it is rare to find two textbooks that agree. They are however definitions that I have found managers understand and can use when managing performance.

Performance management practice and the working environment

Performance management techniques are transferable. They are relevant and necessary in any line management role in any business sector. Chapter 13 explains this.

Case studies

At the end of each chapter we will consider the relevance of the points made by reference to three characters. They all work for a company that delivers its business through six remote branch sites. Other details are:

- 300 staff work in the six branches.

- Each branch has a branch manager.

- Each branch manager has three direct reports (assistant managers) and six indirect reports (supervisors).

- The six branch managers report into a network director based at the company's head office.

Jill -'the Personnel specialist'

Jill is a bright and highly motivated Personnel specialist. She joined the company with a specific brief from the network director to introduce performance management processes. The objective is to improve the efficiency and productivity of the 300 branch based employees. Some old job descriptions exist but nobody refers to them. Jill has been with the company for six months.

Jim -'the conscientious'

Jim is one of the six branch managers. He has worked for the company for twenty years. He joined the company as a junior and has been promoted on four occasions within the same unit. He is a good technician who believes he understands all the tasks others have to complete. He has never received any management training but 'has learned as he has gone along'. Jim's support staff have been trained and promoted by Jim over the years and tend to mirror his style.

Jim is expected to meet a number of job objectives each year including a contribution to profit figure. He is given a 'pay pot' each year and is solely responsible for its distribution among his senior staff. Other staff receive company agreed pay increases. No senior staff have left over recent years but wastage rates in more junior staff are above the company and industry averages.

Jim has just been given his 'contribution to profit' target for the next twelve months and believes it to be unrealistic. He is keen to meet all his job objectives but he is particularly concerned about one objective which calls for a reduction in staff wastage rates.

The network director describes Jim as a solid, intelligent and reliable fellow who is good with customers and technically sound.

Bert - 'keep everyone happy'

Bert is another of the six branch managers. He has worked for the company for 15 years and last year was promoted into his current role from a head office position in public relations. Technically he is comparatively weak but the company believes his inter personal skills are good and customers will like him. Bert has never managed a team of people but believes he can motivate staff without any problem.

Bert believes his job is about keeping everyone happy. However he tends to have 'favourites' and the senior support staff have already noticed he can be less than open. Bert will 'sideline' anyone he does not like, avoiding confrontation.

Bert has also received his job objectives for the ensuing 12 months and presumes they are reasonable.

- 1 -
Practising performance management

This book is concerned with the knowledge and skills managers need to develop to achieve their job objectives through staff. For example, a manager of a sales outlet may have a job objective 'to sell 1000 home insurance policies in the next twelve months'. How does he or she prepare staff to help ensure this objective is achieved? What can be done if the objective is not being met? These are the types of issue addressed in this book.

Managing performance is a manager's responsibility

It is the clear responsibility of the manager to deal with staff performance problems. It is not acceptable for him or her to dismiss problems with expressions like:

- 'This person has a negative attitude and needs to do another job.'

- 'This person has no motivation.'

- 'This person cannot do the job.'

- 'This person needs to go on another training course.'

- 'Personnel will have to deal with this.'

Managers must become competent performance management practitioners. They should be able to deal with the vast majority of staff performance problems. Personnel departments exist to support managers; not to do the manager's job.

Defining performance management practice

An effective performance manager understands performance management practice to be:

- 'Helping someone help himself or herself *improve* or *develop performance.*'

This is what a performance manager should be doing in practice.

- *Improve* refers to someone who is not yet meeting the requirements of their current job.

- *Develop* refers to someone who is meeting the requirements of their current job and is being developed for a larger or different role.

- *Performance* means carrying out actions efficiently and effectively to meet agreed job objectives. Defining 'good' or 'poor' performance over a given period is quite a complex matter and a chapter is devoted to the subject later in the book.

The definition also recognises the responsibility of the individual. Performance Management should be explained as a contract between the manager and the member of staff.

Identifying responsibilities

The manager undertakes to:

- Explain the requirements of the job. The expected outputs and job content.

- Train and to coach the member of staff.

- Provide information and opportunities to gain useful experience.

- Encourage and to monitor and control the staff member's performance.

The member of staff undertakes to:

- Accept the manager's description of the job.

- Listen and to make every effort to learn.

- Undertake willingly jobs for which training has been given.

- Exercise self discipline, for example, meeting deadlines.

Effective performance managers satisfy the above definition. They can and do exist without formal performance management systems.

Performance management systems

This book is primarily concerned with performance management practice. Performance management systems need to be tailored to suit the particular requirements of an organisation. However, system and practice are inextricably linked.

Performance management systems tend to observe the following stages:

Stage one
- A clear statement of the organisation's objectives.

Financial and numerical objectives are relatively easy to express and measure:

- profit targets

- sales volumes

- cost control

- reduction in staff numbers, etc.

Other objectives are less easily measured such as:

- respect for staff

- providing excellent customer service

- adopting open style management.

These 'objectives' are perhaps better described as corporate 'aims'. Their achievement or otherwise is heavily reliant on effective performance management practice.

Stage two
- They record the outputs of jobs across an organisation which should contribute to the achievement of the organisation's objectives.

At this stage an organisation demonstrates the importance of staff contributing to the achievement of its objectives. When performance management systems first became popular it was possible to compare corporate objectives with job objectives and struggle to find a connection. Companies with large work forces in comparatively uncompetitive markets could achieve financial objectives with staff 'firing on three cylinders'. The situation today is very different. Organisations are now more heavily reliant on the productivity levels of individuals and this stage is usually completed very thoroughly.

Stage three
- Job contents are clearly articulated, preferably down to task level and reflect best practice.

Organisations can often fail to address this stage adequately. In an uncoordinated fashion they rely on line management to tell staff what is required. Articulating job contents must be a co-ordinated exercise if staff carrying out the same jobs are to receive the same information. Performance management problems will be the inevitable outcome of devoting insufficient effort to this stage. This is discussed fully in the next chapter 'defining the job'.

Stage four
- Documentation is simple.

A performance management system is intended to help a manager practice performance management more effectively. If the documentation is complex too much time will be devoted to its completion. This results in performance management being perceived as a form filling exercise rather than a process for improving staff performance.

Organisations must avoid the temptation to overload performance management systems. Systems should not be expected to provide data or information unrelated to the performance management process.

The documentation should be capable of recording the information referred to under stage five.

Stage five
- Job goals are recorded, formal reviews and their outcomes are recorded and an annual performance report is produced.

These records reveal:

- What the manager, in this context the appraiser, wants the member of staff, the appraisee, to achieve over the period.

- How well the appraisee is doing and the help being provided by the manager.

- How often performance is being formally reviewed.

- Goal achievement and the individual's progress and training needs.

Stage six
- The appraiser, the appraisee and the appraiser's 'boss' all comment on the annual report.

The appraiser and the appraisee discuss the content of the report and record their feelings. An appraisee's comments can often reveal how well the appraiser has met his or her responsibilities. If the appraisee feels much of the report is unfair or promised support has not been delivered, someone needs to take some action. Many reports cater for this by ensuring the appraiser's boss also sees the report and formally adds comments.

Stage seven
- Appraisees can register a 'failure to agree' with the appraiser's rating and an arbitration procedure exists.

In many organisations appraisees can pursue a formal procedure if they are not satisfied with the outcome of stage six. This will often involve trade union representation, senior line management and Personnel.

Developing performance management practice

Practice is the key
Appraisees' comments on staff reports rarely concern the formalised, performance management system. More commonly they indicate the quality of the performance management relationship with their manager. Their comments highlight the failure of the manager to carry out performance management practice effectively:

- 'I was very surprised to be marked down on customer service. Nothing has ever been said to me.'

- 'I do not accept that I should be marked down on sales results; selling is not my job.'

- 'If I had received the training as promised my performance rating would have been better.'

We can all probably recall examples of appraisees feeling a performance report is unfair. The vast majority of these reactions are a direct result of poor performance management practice. Very few appraisees irrationally reject genuine judgements of their performance.

Systems are not the answer
No performance management system can make up for poor performance management practice. However, good performance management practice can compensate for an inadequate system. A craftsman with a blunt chisel will make a better cabinet than an enthusiastic novice will with all the tools in the world! Good performance managers existed long before someone designed the first performance management system.

A performance management system should therefore be viewed as a 'vehicle' for formally recording good performance management practice in a standardised way.

Blaming the system
The inextricable link between system and practice leads some organisations to blame

the system when problems arise. Before coming to this conclusion organisations should review the knowledge and skill levels of its management. Is poor management practice the real issue?

Some organisations will strive to find a 'system' cure for a 'practice' ill. As mentioned above we should view the system as a 'vehicle' for recording good practice. If a car driver kept having accidents, how many times would you change the car before checking his or her driving knowledge and skills? The tendency to find 'system' fixes rather than address skill problems is a temptation we can all fall into. Poor golfers who change golf clubs each year are seeking a system cure for what may well be a knowledge or skill problem.

Case studies

Jill introduces a performance management system

As directed Jill has been working on her brief to improve staff effectiveness. She has decided to introduce a performance management system. She has designed and produced:

- a start of year objective setting pro forma

- quarterly review record forms

- a training need report form to be completed half yearly

- an end of year performance report form

- a glossy guide on 'how to set objectives'

- a list of training courses available externally

- a self development pro forma to be completed quarterly by everyone

- a one day conference to introduce the process to the branch managers

- a manual describing the company's disciplinary procedure.

Jill believes the branch managers will be able to 'cascade' the information through the line to their staff. She is delighted with her efforts to support the company achieve its goal of improved efficiency and productivity. Having now run the one day conference she is reasonably satisfied with the reaction of the branch managers apart from Jim!

Jim remains to be convinced

Jim just cannot see the point of all the extra paperwork. He cannot see its relevance to improving efficiency or productivity and said so at the one day conference. Jim believes his colleagues felt exactly the same but lacked the bravery to say so to someone 'from head office'.

However Jim prides himself on his professionalism and despite his grumbles he has set about reading all the material.

Bert responds superficially
Bert enjoyed the conference and thought the materials issued were very attractively produced. He will get around to reading and understanding the documentation when he has a moment.

Case studies - Commentary

Despite Jill's hard work the system she has introduced will not in itself produce the desired outcomes of improved efficiency and productivity because:

- Apart from some out of date job descriptions there is no other information about the jobs staff should be completing to meet their job objectives. To expect the branch managers to complete this stage of the process without greater support is not reasonable. Issuing a glossy guide that defines objectives in some abstract sense is of little use. The branch managers need support and guidance if they are to complete the real life exercise effectively.

- The branch staff at all levels complete the same jobs albeit in six outlets. Efficiency and productivity will only be improved if job contents are defined in a coordinated fashion and best practice identified.

- Evidence indicates that Bert and Jim need training if they are to meet their performance management responsibilities in practice. If there is no 'practice' the introduction of a performance management system intended to formalise the practice is an expensive waste of time.

We will return to Jill, Jim and Bert at the end of each chapter. We will observe how Jim and Bert react to new initiatives, as Jill strives to meet her objective.

Points to consider

1. If you were Jill, what plan of action would you have devised to meet the objective of improving the efficiency and productivity of branch staff?

2. How has Jill's work helped to improve the daily, performance management

practices of Jim and Bert?

3. Do you appraise the performance of staff ? Does someone else appraise your performance? Consider how these activities could be improved.

- 2 -
Defining the job – Step one

The 'seven steps' framework enables the user to analyse a performance management issue in a logical sequence. The framework starts with the more common reasons for non performance, or under performance, and finishes up with the least common reasons.

Explaining requirements clearly

Failing to define the job adequately is the most common cause of performance problems. Basically the manager has failed to explain his or her requirements clearly enough. It is simply not good enough to expect employees to muddle along without direction and then criticise them for failing to achieve something that they were never asked to do!

Example
If we want a shop to deliver a new washing machine we ensure we explain:

- The type of washing machine we want delivered.

- The date and time we want to receive the delivery.

- Where we live and, often, how to get there.

We will all have experienced occasions when even the most explicit instructions fail to achieve the desired result. Failure is even more likely if our instructions are vague or non existent. The more we 'want' something to happen the more precise we are with our instructions.

Example
If we want a particular television programme recorded whilst we are out we will ensure the person expected to do the recording knows:

- the title of the programme

- the TV channel

- the start and finish time

- the tape to be used (checking there is enough room on the tape)

- how important it is to us that the programme is recorded
- whatever other tasks the person is doing our recording need comes first.

Written reminders
In addition to expressing our requirement orally we would probably leave written reminders. These may be placed on the television or elsewhere. If we wanted more than one programme recorded it is almost certain that we would support our request with a written reminder. We would certainly not leave the house simply saying, 'please record those programmes we like whilst we are out'

Explaining job requirements adequately
The need for precise instructions is just as important at work. However, managers can often fail to accurately articulate what it is they require from their staff. Stating the objective (output) we want the individual to achieve is half the job. We must also explain adequately what actions (**tasks** or inputs) the individual needs to complete to meet the objective. The decision about how to achieve the objective should not be left to the member of staff. This inevitably results in inefficiency and constant reinvention.

Staff productivity
Such a situation becomes increasingly unacceptable in organisations that rely heavily on high staff productivity levels. In these organisations **task checklists** are often used. They record important, standard tasks that are completed on a regular basis and ensure the tasks reflect best practice.

Using task checklists

When compiling a task checklist the writer should include a measure (a target or a standard) and a time-scale. Tasks, as with objectives, need to be precise not vague. In managing staff performance on a day to day basis 'tasks' tend to be discussed rather than 'higher level' job objectives. Performance managers need to concentrate on inputs if the outputs are to be achieved.

Example
In a customer service business one of the manager's job aims would probably be:

- 'To ensure that all customers receive a warm welcome on arrival.'

None of us would dispute the desirability of such an aim. However, when the manager wants to check out whether this aim is being achieved, some form of task has to be completed. The task to be carried out by the manager may well be prescribed. He or she may be asked to:

- 'Ask six customers per week how they feel they are welcomed on arrival. Record their comments and a brief note of actions taken.'

Such a task may be deemed best practice at a particular point in time. As better practices are identified the task should be amended or replaced.

Managing the 'ways' as well as the 'whats'

The customer service example above highlights the need for performance managers to recognise their responsibility for the 'way' staff complete the 'whats'.

Let us assume, in the above example, responses from customers indicated that some felt they did not receive a 'warm' welcome. The manager must help the staff address the problem. Often managers feel uncomfortable about tackling what they see to be personality issues. They will say things like:

- 'That is typical of Fred who is efficient but does not smile enough.'
- 'That is just his way, he does not mean to come across as rude.'
- 'She has always been like that but I cannot get her to leave.'

These are not acceptable explanations. A performance manager must address these shortcomings as openly as possible.

The key is to explain job responsibilities clearly at the outset. Explain that the job is not limited to completing tasks efficiently; the 'way' the tasks are completed is just as important. From personal experience as 'customers' everyone will recognise this is true. The 'way' we feel we are treated is often as important as the satisfactory completion of the transaction itself.

Example

Christmas was looming and Ian had not sorted out a present for his wife. Time was running out so he left work early and travelled to a local, large shopping centre. Ian entered a department store with some anxiety as he dislikes shopping intensely. He walked, rather uncomfortably, towards the perfumery counter.

On arrival at the counter Ian was immediately greeted by a very well groomed, statuesque lady who politely enquired whether she could be of assistance. In a rather garbled fashion Ian explained he wanted to buy something for his wife for Christmas. The lady assistant asked how much money he was intending to spend. He was in fact trying to buy a present for Christmas morning and had not intended spending a great deal on this particular purchase. However Ian was already feeling somewhat uncomfortable and inflated his intended spend by 50%!

The assistant expertly referred to her product range and brought forth the one product that was within the price range Ian had quoted. She apologised for not being able to offer him a greater choice but this simply added to his discomfort.

Ian thanked the assistant for her help and said he would bear the product in mind. Feeling the cheeks of his face on fire he turned and left the store feeling even more uncomfortable.

If we examine 'what' the shop assistant did we produce a very positive picture:

- She was immediately available on Ian's arrival at the counter.

- Her appearance was very impressive and she welcomed Ian politely.

- She gave Ian her undivided attention and asked a series of clear and logical questions.

- She knew her product range and very efficiently selected a product within Ian's stated cost limit.

Why then did Ian feel as he did? Because the assistant did not recognise Ian's anxiety and therefore failed to adapt her behaviour accordingly.

Supervising the 'way' staff complete tasks

A supervisor observing the above transaction might well have spotted Ian's discomfort. The supervisor should help the shop assistant deal with the next anxious male shopper in a different 'way'. If it was not practicable to give guidance immediately, it should be provided as soon as possible. When dealing with the 'way' staff complete tasks the incident needs to be easily recalled if lessons are to be learned. There is little if any value in simply making a note of an incident and raising it months later in some formal review.

Offering criticism

Asking staff to change behaviour will involve criticism. Performance managers must have created an environment in which the giving and receiving of criticism is understood. Criticism is dealt with in Chapter 6.

Demonstrating empathy develops trust

Performance managers cannot just complete a logical process when managing an individual's performance. The interaction should demonstrate empathy, which in turn develops trust.

When managers turn to their 'boss' to discuss a problem they are seeking an empathetic response. Sadly it is true to say that when turning to their subordinates, managers can often forget others like to be treated similarly. At regular intervals managers should reflect on the 'way' they deal with subordinates. Equally organisations must recognise that only skilled managers will be sufficiently self assured to review the 'way' they carry out the 'whats'. The unskilled manager's sole concern will be meeting deadlines and filling in forms.

Staff will generally accept the intervention of a manager if it is done in the right 'way.' Indeed once staff believe the manager always strives to intervene in the right way they will forgive those occasions when he or she fails!

Constructing task statements

'Step one' is therefore about producing meaningful and measurable task statements that reflect best practice. They will help the jobholder achieve his or her output objectives.

Examples of task statements
The following task statements allow for the inclusion of a measure (target or standard) and a time-scale:

- Conducting a set number of interviews in a given period.

- Meeting sales to interviews ratios in a given period.

- Controlling overtime costs within budget on a monthly basis.

- Meeting deadlines for returns.

- Meeting error ratios in form completion.

- Meeting training schedules.

- Completing performance reviews to set standards and as scheduled.

- Meeting laid down dress standards.

- Holding regular and effective meetings as scheduled.

- Maintaining business leads registers on a daily basis.
- Undertaking 'mailshots' as scheduled and meeting volume targets.
- Meeting cross sales ratios in a given period.
- Logging (number of) future business opportunities daily.
- Responding to customer complaints in the required time-scale.
- Meeting customer contact targets by agreed deadlines.
- Debriefing staff performance as scheduled.
- Maintaining accurate interview notes on the completion of each interview.
- Meeting external visiting schedules.
- Review punctuality standards weekly and address any problems.
- Branch appearance standards reviewed daily.
- Number of cash errors not to exceed (number) in a given period.
- Meeting after sales service standards and deadlines.
- Reviewing health and safety and security standards on a (time-scale) basis.

This list of tasks illustrates how job requirements can be broken down into statements to which a target or standard and time-scale can be added. It is possible to compare staff carrying out similar jobs because many of the tasks are measured in a common way. The tasks include time-scales, ratios and company standards.

Writing task checklists-commitment
To most busy managers the thought of articulating job requirements so precisely is a nightmare. Therefore before embarking on such a laborious exercise the manager needs to consider a number of questions:

- 'Is success heavily dependent on the production of individuals?'
- 'Do I seem to spend all my time repeating instructions to staff?'
- 'Am I always chasing people who miss time-scales?'
- 'Do I have a lot of inexperienced staff?'
- 'Do I have to explain things that are common sense?'
- 'Do I lose my temper because staff are so inefficient?'
- 'Are there tasks that are never quite completed properly?'

If the answers to these questions are in the main 'yes', then before looking for the problem elsewhere, we need to establish how well we have:

- described our requirements

- communicated our priorities

- identified best practice.

Producing task statements

It is neither practicable nor sensible to seek to document every last task someone completes. This will only bury people in paper. However, neither is it sensible nor fair to leave staff without adequate direction. There is an optimum middle ground and with a little bit of trial and error the performance manager will find the optimum approach.

There are three approaches to producing task statements:

1. Rely on explaining the task orally and the staff member remembering the requirements. Rely on memory when discussing performance.

2. Select a few key/important tasks.
   - Discuss the requirements and write them down.
   - Refer to the written record when discussing performance.
   - Rely on method 'one' for the other tasks.
   - Add to the written record over a period of time if method 'one' does not seem to be working.

3. Select as many key/important tasks as you can.
   - Discuss the requirements and write them down.
   - Refer to the written record when discussing performance.
   - Add to/delete from the written record as necessary.
   - Address any problems in the completion of other tasks orally as they arise.

Irrespective of the option chosen 'best practice' should be introduced as identified.

Choosing an option
The option selected should suit the business requirements.

Example
A manager with many inexperienced staff carrying out the same job in different locations may choose option three, because:

- The manager will be able to monitor and control performance more easily.

- Best practice will be introduced more efficiently.

- Inexperienced staff will very much welcome the clarity provided by the checklists.

Conversely a sole trader employing one person may well select option 'one' as the most cost effective approach.

The size of a business and the extent of its network will inevitably influence the option chosen. However, if managing the performance of individuals and their productivity levels is seen as important, one option must be chosen.

Providing direction
Job holders given no direction will decide what the job is about; its priorities and measurements.

Example
You have purchased a sweet shop next to a school. You intend the shop to open each morning at 8.15 a.m. How would you react if the person employed to run the shop did not let customers in until 9.00 a.m.? The 'job description', if one existed, may not specifically state the daily opening time. You would very quickly correct this omission by stating that the shop must be open at 8.15 a.m. You might also state that you expect:

- the opening time of 8.15 a.m.(the target)

- to be met 95% of the time (the standard)

- over any calendar month (the time-scale).

You will have produced a task statement. You would also produce task statements if you found:

- 'out of date' products in the store room

- empty product shelves

- dirty display cabinets

Managers should think about their area of operation as their 'shop'. When they think in this way they recognise it is their responsibility to provide direction. They recognise the need to be explicit about tasks.

Staff want to succeed
It is true to say that the vast majority of employees want to do a good job. They want to carry out tasks satisfactorily. It is managers failing to ensure job requirements are clear and understood that is often the problem.

Regularly reviewing step one

A manager must regularly return to step one to maintain this common understanding of job requirements. Step one is the foundation upon which all other performance management activity stands or falls. Time devoted to the maintenance of job requirements is time well spent.

If job objectives (outputs) change, so will the job's content (tasks or inputs). Tasks historically seen as important can become redundant and be deleted. Some tasks not highlighted in the checklist can grow in importance and be added. Checklists must therefore be seen as 'live' documents. Management must in the end determine the percentage of a job's total tasks that are to be recorded in this way. The remainder are then dealt with orally on an 'as necessary' basis.

Case studies

Jill assesses the success of the objective setting exercise
Jill reviewed the completion of the objective setting pro formas in the six branches. She was very disappointed with the findings. People employed in the same job role seemed to have different objectives. The number of objectives varied tremendously from branch to branch. The glossy guide on 'how to set objectives' had either not worked or had been ignored. Jill recognised that there was a good deal of work to be done if the performance management system was to be anything but a meaningless, form filling chore.

Jill decided to tackle the problems by:

- Providing technical support to the network director to enable him to detail the job objectives of his six direct reports- the branch managers.

- Helping the branch management produce job objectives for branch staff.

- Explaining the importance of 'step one' to the branch managers.

- Gaining the branch managers' commitment to a detailed review of what staff were actually doing everyday in branches - including the branch managers themselves.

- Analysing the outputs of the above actions with the network director and the branch managers.

- Supporting the company produce meaningful and precise job objectives, descriptions and 'task checklists'.

Jim is looking for support

Jim did not find the objective setting exercise easy. He thought he had explained it reasonably well to his own line management but none had found it easy to 'dream up' objectives that had never existed before. The glossy brochure had talked about objectives in a rather theoretical way. He could find no examples relevant to his business. The fact that Jill was now getting the company to explain more clearly what it wanted seemed a good idea. Jim often grumbled that he was given a profit objective that went up every year and he was left to get on with it. If Jim raised queries the network director invariably responded by telling Jim to 'go away and manage it'. Jim took this to mean that the network director had no useful suggestions.

Jim was getting increasingly anxious about achieving his profit objective and welcomed Jill's ideas. He accepted identifying best practice would help. Jim felt his staff would find it easy to explain the tasks they carried out. He was confident that he and his line management would be able to add quality and quantity measures and time-scales. He was pretty sure other branch managers would copy his findings.

Bert abdicates responsibility

Bert had passed responsibility for the objective setting exercise to his own line management and was disappointed to learn of Jill's findings. However if head office wanted all branch jobs to be reviewed he was happy for this to happen. He would ensure all the material was with Jill by the deadline set.

Case studies - Commentary

Jill has now addressed two of the three points raised in the 'case studies commentary' at the end of chapter one. Jill now needs to:

- Work with the network director to produce clear job objectives for the branch managers.

- Help the branch managers produce clear objectives for other branch staff.

- Find out what is actually going on in the branches.

The input from the branches will require the management team to:

- Agree the task content of jobs.

- Define the standards, targets and time-scales that should be measures of effectiveness.

- Agree the proportion of a job's content that should be recorded on 'task checklists'.

- Identify the 'important' tasks that will have to be recorded.

- Recognise the exercise is not a 'one off' but something that will have to be regularly repeated.

Subsequently Jim and Bert will have to manage the performance of their staff to meet the task requirements. At this stage Jim and Bert will need training in the practice of performance management.

The network director will have to meet with his managing director to agree the job objectives of the branch managers. The branch manager's job content will then need to be agreed with the branch managers. Over a period of time the job content will need to be refined as necessary.

The network director will have to chair a meeting or series of meetings with his branch managers. These meetings will result in the production of common task statements for each job in the branches. Measures of effectiveness will then be added to the statements. Jill should be part of these meetings because she is responsible for the successful implementation of the performance management system.

Until the groundwork is completed Jill should suspend the formal performance management system. In due course the system will need to be reintroduced effectively.

Points to consider

1. Do your staff see the priorities of their jobs in the way you do? Ask them to write down, from one to ten, the most important tasks they feel they complete on a regular basis. If you have never completed this exercise you will be surprised by what you discover.

2. List five 'important' tasks you complete regularly. Add a standard or target measure and a time-scale. If your boss has explained your job to you clearly you should find this easy. It does not matter whether the tasks are written down or not.

3. Think about two occasions when you were a customer and you felt you were dealt with in the wrong 'way'. Select occasions when the 'whats' were completed satisfactorily.

4. Have you ever avoided raising a 'way' issue with a member of your staff? If so, why?

- 3 -
Providing job related training – Step two

A performance manager cannot establish effective job related training programmes unless step one has been completed thoroughly. Step two deals with the knowledge and skills staff must acquire to meet their job requirements.

Defining job related training

Job related training explains how *theories* and *systems* can be applied in *practice*.

Example
Engineers required to install air conditioning systems may well receive training that:

- Explains how *theoretically* air can be conditioned.

- Describes the air conditioning *system* their company has designed and manufactured.

- Teaches them how to install the system in *practice*.

The theory and system training is important. However it is of no practical use if the engineer cannot install the system in practice.

Example
If we purchase a radio we are not particularly interested in the theories behind radio communication. Few of us would be interested in the precise internal construction of the radio. However if there are no instructions on how to fit the batteries or tune the radio in to a particular station, we will not be able to use radio in practice.

Therefore training people in theories and systems has to be supported by effective job related training. That is, how to use the *system* to apply the *theory* in *practice*.

Establishing the importance of job related training

If job requirements are clear, job related training programmes can be precise and cost effective.

It is still common to witness training programmes being cancelled or postponed when work pressures are high. This is often the result of those programmes failing to demonstrate that they will improve the everyday performance of the work-force. The decision to cancel or postpone most job related training is taken by line management. Other work is given priority. This will not happen if managers can see a direct relationship between time expended on training staff, with an efficiency or productivity return.

Delivering training

Many organisations have their own training departments and residential colleges. They exist to support the performance manager meet his or her training responsibilities. However this more specialist support rarely deals with the daily, job related training needs of staff. It tends to concentrate on the theory and system training described above. Job related training is the everyday responsibility of the performance manager.

There are various techniques for delivering on job training but they all rely upon the completion of 'step one'.

Job related training

Preparatory training
Preparatory training is training a new entrant or someone about to assume new responsibilities. If job requirements are clear this should be a reasonably straightforward exercise.

Example
Someone recruited to work on a post office counter needs to know how to:

- count cash

- issue road fund licences

- complete standard forms

- keep records, etc.

A new employee cannot function without this basic training. Therefore most organisations have in place sound, basic training programmes for new entrants.

Organisations tend to be less thorough when preparing staff for greater responsibility. For example, someone about to assume responsibility for staff needs to be trained in the techniques of performance management. However it is still common to see organisations failing to provide adequate supervisory training. If 'step one' is completed thoroughly this oversight can be avoided.

Maintaining knowledge and skill levels

Most managers recognise the need for initial or preparatory training to enable staff to complete new tasks. However some do not regularly check and maintain knowledge and skill levels. If we fill up a car engine with oil we do not assume the engine will never need 'topping up'. We will regularly check the oil level or get someone else to do it. Staff who have received and benefited from effective preparatory training have a similar need. Their knowledge and skill levels should be checked on a regular basis and the levels 'topped up' as necessary.

Remedial training

This training is intended to overcome a problem in a person's performance despite that person having received preparatory training. It assumes the performance manager has assessed the individual's problem accurately. Further training is not always the solution. We will see in subsequent chapters that remedial training is often incorrectly selected as the 'cure'. This happens because the underlying ill has not been diagnosed accurately. However if the problem is identified correctly and can be satisfactorily addressed by repeat training, this option should be selected. For example, a cashier may be experiencing problems with counting cash correctly. The answer is to train the cashier to adopt a technique which is less prone to error.

Best practice

Prescribing the vast majority of tasks is in some businesses a necessity. This is the case in any mass production industry.. Computerisation has forced many other organisations to ensure staff carry out certain tasks in a standard way. Whether they are sales people, cashiers or shop workers, standard tasks are prescribed. However identifying best practice should not be limited to tasks that are determined by system requirements. Good performance managers identify best practice wherever it occurs and ensure it is adopted by all staff completing the same job.

When a best practice is identified it can be recorded and others trained to adopt it. The benefits of training staff to adopt best practice would seem obvious, but it involves removing 'choice'. Training of this nature has to be introduced carefully if it is to be successful. Subsequent chapters in this book explain why this is the case.

Job rotation

In some organisations staff will enjoy the same job title and job description but for operational reasons specialise in one part of the job. To ensure all staff become familiar with the whole job it is common for organisations to encourage job rotation.

Performance managers are expected to ensure job rotation is in place. In reality this form of training needs to be closely monitored to ensure it happens. Clear job requirements are a necessity.

Job enlargement/job enrichment

Job enlargement simply means training someone to undertake more tasks as part of their daily duties. Job enrichment is about training staff to assume greater responsibility for the tasks they undertake. In both cases the need for clear job requirements is plain if the attendant training is to be effective.

Assessing knowledge and skill levels

Knowledge

Managers must regularly assess knowledge levels. They must establish whether an individual's knowledge is sufficiently sound to meet the job's requirements. The first step would be to establish whether the individual has satisfactorily completed the preparatory training. Clearly if this stage has been missed it needs to be completed before going any further. If the preparatory training has been completed knowledge levels can be checked out by:

- asking questions on a 'one to one' basis

- oral or written tests.

These techniques are helpful if the concern is about things like:

- product information

- facts and figures, for example, interest rates

- knowing the correct procedure

- knowing where to refer problems.

Programmed learning

If knowledge levels are inadequate then the individual needs to receive the necessary training. It is often more effective for the individual to improve his or her knowledge levels by reading materials specifically designed to improve knowledge. Programmed learning material that presents information in an easily digestible fashion and allows for self testing can be very effective.

Skill

A good deal of training at work is intended to improve an individual's skills:

- selling techniques

- interviewing techniques

- leadership skills

- answering the telephone

- greeting customers.

In these areas it is not enough to test knowledge, the manager must assess the related skill.

Example

To explain the relationship, and the difference, between *knowledge* and *skill* we will consider an average golfer's swing.

The average, enthusiastic golfer's *knowledge* of technique is often sound. They are avid readers of books and magazines. If their knowledge is tested they will appear to be capable golfers. However, observation of the golfer's actual golf swing will prove that most keen, average golfers are educated duffers! Despite a great deal of knowledge the average golfer cannot develop the *skills* to produce low scores.

Skill can be checked out by a combination of:

- one to one role plays

- observation on the job

- analysis of results. These could be sales results or error ratios.

Analysing results raises questions. Poor results should lead the performance manager to ask questions. Observing on the job performance or completing role plays is how skill levels can be checked.

Training removes fear

In later chapters we will explore in more detail the issues of motives and motivation. However, when establishing whether a performance problem is a training issue performance managers must appreciate the power of a motive that is common to us all. That motive is the *fear* or *self preservation* motive.

Understanding the 'fear' or 'self preservation' motive.

Most of us are employed in jobs where the threat of physical violence is not a feature. However we still *fear* the unknown, failure, looking stupid, etc. Everyone can probably remember how they felt on their first day at a new school or their first day at work. That feeling of apprehension that most of us experience when we do not know what to expect. *Fear* is a motive we feel instinctively and respond to as our personality dictates. Some people respond aggressively whereas others seek to 'get away' from the situation.

When managers ask staff to try something new or to change a way of doing things they must cater for the fear motive. It is important to understand that even the most willing and open minded person will feel apprehensive. This is why preparatory training and on job coaching are so vital. They give the willing employee confidence. Fear is removed. If preparatory training and on job coaching follow up are missing, fear will not have been removed.

Coaching and training is an everyday activity

If we recognise the importance of preparatory training, then the need for refresher training and coaching should be equally obvious. In our everyday life we will undertake some tasks infrequently:

- changing a film in a camera
- putting batteries in a toy
- servicing the lawn mower

Whilst we read the instructions the last time we will want to read them again. This is a form of job related refresher training or, if someone shows us, coaching. Staff who receive adequate preparatory training can become 'rusty'. They feel less confident about undertaking a particular job or task. Often they do not recognise this for themselves.

Because of the strength of the 'self preservation' motive in all of us the manager needs to be confident that 'step two' is dealt with thoroughly. If training is not thorough staff will not perform properly. The manager must be confident that the problem is not a training issue before exploring other avenues dealt with in subsequent chapters.

Case studies

Jill introduces a review of training needs

Jill has now completed the four action points set out at the end of the last chapter.

The training needs emerging from the exercise now have to de documented. A training programme has to be costed and agreed with line management. Jill recognises that with so many training needs priorities will have to be established. In discussions with the network director and the branch managers it is agreed that training activity should concentrate on the following:

- The introduction of best practice across all jobs.

- Performance management practice training for all line management.

- Raising the performance of all staff to meet the standards, targets and time-scales of the most efficient staff.

Jim recognises the need for training

Jim had always thought he knew the requirements of his job. However recent events have demonstrated he is not doing enough to develop his own line management. In addition he needs training personally to help him manage people and their performance more effectively. He was disappointed with the results of the 'audit' of the activities of his staff as he was certain he had told them what was required.

Jim recognises the logic behind the exercise. He has started agreeing training plans for all his staff. He knows the priority is to ensure his staff adopt the best practices agreed at recent meetings. His staff will also need to meet the time-scales, standards and targets, that are now 'company' measures.

Jim concludes much of the training can be completed 'on the job' by his own team. He explained to Jill that he would be looking for help in those areas outside his competence which tended to revolve around staff management issues.

Bert begins to understand his job

Bert was staggered by all that had gone on in recent weeks. It was as though he had now joined a new organisation. He had no idea that his own job was so complex let alone the jobs of his staff. He was disappointed to find that his staff above all others needed to meet tighter time-scales, higher standards and stiffer targets. He recognises though that staff in other branches are meeting these requirements so his staff are not being treated unreasonably.

Bert is pleased that he has been paired with Jim by Jill. She has suggested that they help each other work through the training need analysis exercise. They could involve her at any time. In addition Bert found his own line management were keen to become involved and this would help.

Case studies – Commentary

With Jill's help and energy the team has come a long way. The foundations are sound and it will now be possible to improve performance management activity as a result. The line management is now armed with clear job objectives, job descriptions and task checklists. This means they can begin to use the formal documentation issued at the time the performance management system was introduced.

Jill now needs to ensure the line management receives effective, job related training in the practice of performance management. Once this is done she can link her performance management system to the practice.

Job related training programmes need to be designed for all other staff to ensure best practice is introduced across the branches. Those staff expected to meet tighter time-scales or higher standards or targets must be shown how. Jill can help by producing training guides, training records and commissioning the writing of programmed learning material to assist with knowledge training.

Jim has welcomed his newly defined responsibilities. Jim is beginning to see how, by getting more out of all his staff, the stiff objectives he has been set can be achieved.

Bert's situation is somewhat different. Having been virtually thrown into the branch manager role without any preparatory training he is beginning to recognise his shortcomings. He will need support and encouragement if his long term suitability for the role of branch manager is to be assessed fairly. Jill has recognised Bert needs help by pairing him with Jim and offering her own support.

Points to consider

1. Have you ever attended a training event and wondered what you were doing there? Why did this happen?

2. Have you ever sent a member of staff on a training event in the hope it would solve a problem?

3. Can you recall being asked to do something for which you felt inadequately prepared? How did you feel? What common motive was operating?

- 4 -
Understanding and influencing attitudes – Step three

Most performance problems managers encounter with 'willing' members of staff will be overcome by:

- Clearly explaining the job's requirements, step one.

- Ensuring adequate preparatory training and follow up training and coaching is provided, step two.

However some staff can appear 'unwilling' to try out newly taught skills and this blockage needs to be explored. The third most common reason for non performance is linked to an individual's 'attitude'.

Defining attitude

The definition used in the context of the 'seven steps' is:

- 'Attitude' is the 'way' we think. It is based on *information* and *experience*. Where these inputs are missing it is based on *assumption*.'

The definition is one managers can work with to improve staff performance.

Developing work related attitudes

Our 'attitude box'

If we recall our first day at work most of us arrived with an 'open mind'. Others arrived with a few superficial attitudes about the job that could be easily influenced . At the end of our first day we would have found our 'attitude box' contained some views about the job that had not been there when we left home. Some attitudes may have felt good, positive, and some may have felt bad, negative, but they would have been based in the main on the *information* received that day and the *experiences* of the day.

As time passed we continued to fill up our 'attitude box.' In addition we revised some of the attitudes already in the 'box'. This happened as we received fresh information or enjoyed fresh experiences. We would have listened to others gossip and added an attitude based on *assumption* to our collection. Whilst we had no first hand information or experience of the topic or person, we would still have formed a view. Then as we received fresh information, experienced new things or heard more gossip, we refined our attitudes.

Our 'work attitude box' has been functioning on this basis ever since.

Identifying a person's attitudes

The simple and clear definition of 'attitude' enables the line manager to construct questions to draw out an individual's views.

Example
A person understands their job is to sell. He or she has been adequately trained and coached, but appears unwilling to sell. The performance manager needs to explore the person's attitude to selling.

- 'What do you think about selling personally?'

- 'Why do you think that?'

- 'What *information* have you received about selling personally?'

- 'What have you heard, been told about selling personally?'- exploring *assumption*.

- 'Have you ever *experienced* selling personally.'

- 'Describe your recent *experiences*.'

The questions are constructed around the key words within the definition; *information, experience* and *assumption*. Attitudes are hidden and to bring them out into the open requires precise questioning. Once attitudes are articulated a line manager can seek to influence them. He or she can provide fresh information or arrange for the individual to undertake a fresh experience.

Reviewing 'steps one and two'

The line manager when listening to responses must be confident that 'steps one and two' have been dealt with adequately.

Example
If a member of staff is 'anti-selling' is this because the person:

- Does not understand selling is part of the job - 'step one'.

- Is fearful of trying to sell because they have not received adequate training - 'step two'.

- Has become fearful because they have not had any recent training or coaching - 'step two'.

Understanding how attitudes influence behaviour

It can help managers appreciate the definition of attitude by talking about how we behave outside work.

We form views on limited information or experience

If we never passed a remark on any topic unless we had reliable information or first hand experience, most everyday conversation would come to an end. People would cease to voice opinions on subjects like football managers, cricket teams, politicians, and world events. Gossip would disappear. Conversations at parties or in pubs would become quite boring.

In our everyday world we all tend to voice views on matters about which we have inadequate information or experience. It makes no sense, however, for performance managers to form views about staff on limited information. Nor is it necessary for staff to form views on aspects of their work in this way. Performance managers must recognise the importance of gathering and providing information. This often requires conscious effort given our 'everyday' behaviour.

Experience is a powerful influence

How often do we hear expressions such as:

- 'It was not as bad as I thought it would be'

- 'I never thought I would be able to do it'

- 'He is not so bad when you get to know him'

- 'I wish I had tried it earlier'

- 'I'm never going to shop there again'

- 'The food was awful; that is the last time I will eat there.'

Some of the expressions are positive and others negative. The performance manager needs to recognise that work experiences are just as powerful. In the negative examples the shop or restaurant is unlikely to be given an opportunity to change the attitude. The situation at work is different. The performance manager has ample opportunity every day to provide fresh, positive experiences.

Maintaining positive attitudes

Managers have to work at maintaining positive attitudes in staff. A positive attitude one day can be negative the next if the individual receives unhelpful information or has a bad experience. Being alert to this potential problem is all that can be reasonably expected. Once identified the manager should however know how to tackle the problem and a clear working definition of 'attitude' very much helps.

Managing our own attitudes

The above deals with the working relationship between a manager and a member of staff when exploring performance issues. However all managers come to work with a whole set of other attitudes and prejudices that are not necessarily work related. These need to be identified and controlled when managing others. This issue is addressed under 'Managers managing themselves' later.

Attitude is sometimes 'step one'

Whilst 'attitude' is the third step when analysing a performance problem, in many circumstances it is the first step. The chapter on 'implementing changes successfully' explains this in more detail, but it is worth giving an example at this stage.

Example
Imagine you were told that your next, urgent job was to leave the first floor room you were occupying:

- You were told to leap into the ornamental pond below - 'step one'.

- You were then shown how to open the window; how to retire four paces and run and leap into the air with your right leg leading - 'step two'.

Would you do what you were asked without question? Highly unlikely. You would probably want to know why you should undertake such a risky exercise. Few people would blindly follow such instructions. However, if you were told the building was going to collapse in thirty seconds, your attitude would form rapidly. This *information* would influence your 'attitude' sufficiently to ensure you carried out the 'job' in the way you had been trained!

Less extreme examples of the power of 'attitude' exist in everyday life:

- Sales people often have a few seconds to influence a potential buyer's 'attitude'. They strive to sell themselves before talking about their products.

- Telephone sellers have the added disadvantage of being physically remote and contacting people without invitation. Few of us answer such telephone calls with an open mind.

To be effective a performance manager must understand the important influence of 'attitudes' on behaviour. He or she must also be able to influence staff attitudes and a working definition is therefore essential.

Case studies

Jill witnesses the power of attitude
Jill is very pleased with the standards now being demonstrated. The setting and recording of job objectives has been completed satisfactorily. The training need pro formas have also been completed well.. The line management now seems to recognise the importance of the whole exercise and the benefits that can be derived.

Jill can see that the managers now accept performance management is part of their jobs. Performance management practice courses have been completed and the managers are gradually learning how to carry out their responsibilities. It is clear that recent experiences have changed their attitudes.

Jim understands he must maintain positive attitudes
Jim is very comfortable applying his newly acquired knowledge and skills. Already he is seeing small successes. By training his most junior staff in half a dozen best practice tasks he has reduced overtime. He has also noticed that the junior staff enjoy the benefit of leaving earlier and are proud that they are completing these tasks as well as anybody. These early experiences have influenced the attitudes of all the staff. People are now asking when they are going to receive their training. What a difference from the time when staff seemed to dread training sessions!

Job related training sessions are scheduled. They are published and all staff can see when they will receive their training. Given the positive reaction to date, Jim informs his own line management that the training sessions must be run as scheduled. Jim recognises that better efficiency will provide time for greater productivity. This will mean he is more likely to achieve his own job objectives. In addition staff are talking to each other in a very positive way about the training sessions and the benefits. Jim knows it is up to him to ensure the training sessions continue if the attitudes of staff are to remain positive.

Bert's attitude is right but he is not happy

With Jim's help, Jill's guidance and the sterling support of his assistant managers, Bert is seeing benefits from all the hard work. Bert attitudinally accepts that performance management is part of his job. He also recognises it is part of the jobs of his own line management. However he cannot say he really enjoys the changed role.

The network director visited the branch and complimented Bert on the progress made to date. The network director was keen to discuss the reactions of staff to the initiatives but Bert was not comfortable talking about his staff on an individual basis. Frankly he had left much of the implementation of the exercise to date to his assistant managers.

When the network director left Bert reflected on his own situation. He knew what his job was; he was receiving training to do the job and he accepted that his experience of the exercise so far was positive. Why then did he feel so dissatisfied and anxious?

Case studies - Commentary

All the branches are currently busy with job related training programmes. The programmes are beginning to deliver success. Jim has clearly taken to his new role well. He is prepared to learn new techniques to help him tackle performance management problems.

Jill has now begun to link performance management practice in the branches with her performance management system. This must happen if the system is to be of any real benefit.

Bert is clearly having doubts about the role he is now being asked to fulfil. At the moment he cannot identify 'why'. The reasons for his doubts will become clearer in subsequent chapters.

Points to consider

1. Think about the last time you influenced a colleague's attitude about a job related matter. Use the questions detailed in this chapter to establish how you did it.

2. Identify two of your own work related attitudes that have changed in the last month. Identify what caused the changes. Did the changes result from fresh *experience*, new *information*, or your making an *assumption*? Was it one of these inputs or a combination of all three?

3. How quickly do you form attitudes and how often do you find they change?

- 5 -
Creating the right working environment – Step four

If we have completed 'steps one to three' effectively we are dealing with someone who:

- Understands the requirements of the job - step one.
- Has been trained and coached to meet the requirements of the job - step two.
- Possesses a willing attitude - step three.

Reasons for non performance at this stage may be found in step four.

Analysing the environment

This step is dealt with in three parts:

- external motivation
- monitoring and control
- self discipline.

External motivation

External motivation is what people do to us to make us behave in a certain way. It is about the techniques organisations and managers employ to motivate staff.

Learning to motivate others
In a retirement speech a manager was heard to say that in nearly thirty years he had met three people to whom he would ascribe that over used word 'charisma'. Most people asked to manage or lead others do not possess 'charisma'. That odd mixture of personality traits that results in staff following them unquestioningly as devoted disciples. Most lesser mortals need to learn the techniques that will result in their motivating others.

Motivating others
Managers employing external motivation techniques assume that specific actions will

encourage the desired staff behaviour. In the main this assumption is correct. We can all remember when a certain behaviour was recognised as 'good' and we were encouraged to repeat it. Equally we can probably remember the converse situation.

Words people associate with motivating others include:

- incentives

- rewards

- recognition

- status

- praise.

People will also recognise the words:

- bullied

- threatened

- intimidated.

These opposite approaches are often summarised as the 'carrot and stick' approach.

The 'stick' approach

We have already recognised under 'step two' that 'self preservation' is probably the strongest motive in all of us. This is why poor managers often rely solely on threat and intimidation to change staff behaviour.

Most organisations deplore bullying and actively seek to eradicate it. Social change and changes in the expectations of employees also work against the bully. This means poor managers who rely solely on threat to 'motivate' staff cannot survive over the long term.

Using the 'fear arrow'

It would be naive though to conclude that managers must never penalise consistently poor performance. Appealing to an individual's 'self preservation' motive is necessary sometimes. It is useful to visualise a manager's motivation techniques as arrows in a quiver. The poor manager has one arrow; the 'fear arrow'. He or she uses this arrow all the time in an aggressive fashion. The good manager has a full quiver of arrows. One of these is the 'fear' arrow. However it is used sparingly.

A manager can appeal to a person's self preservation motive in an adult fashion. There is no need for bullying. Explaining calmly that a person will face this or that sanction if undesired behaviour continues is an inevitable part of working life.

The 'carrot' approach

The 'carrot' aspect of external motivation requires the manager to understand the complexity of internal motivation. Internal motivation is about the needs and wants we personally feel we need to satisfy. It is unique in each of us and changes over time and in different circumstances.

Example

A manager has returned from a training course on external motivation. He has learned a new way of motivating staff to behave just as managers would wish.

The revolutionary technique is to make a chocolate cake to a secret recipe and to feed the cake to staff once a week.

The manager bakes the cake and asks his eight members of staff to line up in front of his office. Seven of the staff respond positively after eating the cake, however the eighth person spits the cake out. The manager concludes that the eighth person must have a problem because the 'motivation' worked in all the other cases. What the manager did not know was that the eighth person had just arrived back from the Sahara Desert. He was in need of a glass of water not chocolate cake!

We could replace 'chocolate cake' in the story with all sorts of devices used to externally motivate staff, such as:

- foreign trips
- theatre outings
- week end breaks
- parties
- free meals in expensive restaurants
- competitions
- league tables
- promotion.

We would still find a minority of people who would not change behaviour as a result of these forms of external motivation.

In the story the manager has failed to recognise the power of internal motivation. If he had given the eighth member of staff a tumbler of water then everyone would have been happy.

Incentive schemes

Incentive schemes are now quite common. Whether they actually result in extra productivity across an entire work force is debatable. What tends to happen is they appeal to many at the outset but only a few ultimately benefit. Those who feel they are too far behind in an annual race for the prize can actually feel demotivated. The favourites tend to be the same people each year. In the end they view incentive schemes as part of their remuneration package.

Competition

Incentives and prizes appeal to the competitive and not everyone is competitive. Those who possess this motive to an extreme degree can even adopt unproductive, short term tactics to secure the prize.

Recognition

Incentive schemes are often deemed to be synonymous with recognition but this is incorrect. Incentive schemes seek to engender the desired behaviour in advance. The reward is known at the outset. The rules of the scheme often leave little room for recognising good performance that does not meet the published rules. Recognition that is unexpected and does not become habitual is a far more powerful tool than annual or regular incentive schemes.

Effective motivators

Understanding external motivation techniques is important. The leader who can apply and link external motivation techniques with an understanding of internal motivation needs will be a very effective 'motivator.'

The best 'motivators' are:

- sincere

- empathetic

- consistent.

Insincere and over used praise at one extreme and the use of unreasonable threats at the other, leave staff feeling confused. If we make a silly mistake because we have been careless we expect some form of reprimand. If we have done something really well we expect praise. Staff like to be able to predict how their manager is likely to react in a given set of circumstances. If a manager is unpredictable, and therefore inconsistent, performance will be affected.

Monitoring and control

Monitoring and control is about managers ensuring staff are meeting job requirements, that:

- targets are being met

- standards are being achieved

- time-scales are being met.

By definition therefore 'step one' must have been completed thoroughly. When managers monitor and control the completion of tasks they are demonstrating that the tasks are important. If you were told a task you completed was important but no one ever mentioned it again, what attitude would you develop?

Monitoring and control and task checklists
Under 'step one' it was stated:

- 'If a manager is concerned with the production levels of individuals, then a task checklist is the most thorough way of ensuring day to day requirements are clearly understood.'

Such a checklist also makes it easier for the manager to monitor and control performance and to select priorities. Managers who do not articulate task requirements thoroughly inevitably become embroiled in sterile debates. They concentrate on the failure to achieve job objectives without establishing reasons for failure.

Discussing task completion (the inputs)

Example
We will return to an example used in chapter two. In that example you asked a family member to record a television programme whilst you were out. If they failed to achieve this objective you could respond in one of two ways.

Concentrating on the lack of output
Dwelling on the non achievement of the objective may make you feel better. You will be able to vent your annoyance. The discussion though is likely to be unproductive. The outcome may well be your storming off saying something like, 'why do I have to do everything myself!'

No lessons are learned because the reasons for failure remain unknown:

- were your instructions unclear?

- did the person lack self discipline and forget?

- did the person just not care?

Concentrating on the inputs

If you had dealt with the task in the detailed fashion explained in chapter two you would be able to establish precisely what went wrong. The discussion would be productive and hopefully avoid a repetition.

Selecting the inputs

Completion of the inputs should therefore form the basis of a discussion on current performance. The manager selects those 'inputs' that need to be discussed from reference to management information on 'outputs':

- sales results

- customer satisfaction surveys

- audit reports

- staff attitude surveys

- error reports

- cost reports.

This management information will raise questions. The discussion should provide the answers. To be productive the discussion must be controlled by the manager. He or she needs to be skilled in the use of debriefing techniques. These techniques are explained in chapter 10.

Addressing a few issues at a time

Monitoring and control meetings should be held frequently and deal with a few points at a time. They are then helpful and productive. These frequent meetings are often subsequently summarised in comprehensive reviews conducted quarterly, half yearly or annually.

'On site' management

'On site' management is where the manager and staff are in one physical location. In this situation monitoring and controlling activity is completed more easily. For example, if the manager observes a member of staff failing to greet customers as required, the failure can be addressed there and then.

'Remote site' management

'Remote site' management is where direct reports are situated in a number of separate physical locations. This situation requires the manager to rely more heavily on paper based information. This will include:

- task checklists or clear statements of job requirements

- the management information referred to above

- third party input

- occasional visits.

'Remote site' managers have to be, by the very nature of the job, effective debriefers of performance. They need to get quickly to the nub of any problem.

Summary

The main requirements for successful monitoring and control activity are:

- Clear job objectives (the outputs).

- A clear statement of job requirements, (the inputs).

- Reliable management information on outputs.

- A manager who can 'debrief' effectively.

- A manager who can analyse responses via the 'seven steps' and show the way forward.

Exercising self discipline

Self discipline is really saying to an individual, 'why do you not monitor and control yourself?' For a number of reasons self discipline will always need to be augmented by some degree of intervention by line management. This intervention can be minimal if someone develops self discipline.

Self discipline needs to be engendered in most people. Monitoring and control, by one's manager, helps engender this quality. Monitoring and control is often about reminding people to carry out their responsibilities as they were trained to do. People can forget or fall into unhelpful habits.

Being professional

You cannot do a professional job without self discipline. Professionals do not require constant intervention from above to:

- keep their technical knowledge up to date

- remain aware of developments in their business area
- take an interest in their market place
- control deadlines
- meet standards and targets or know why they are not being met
- keep others informed
- institute remedial action.

Most people expect professional behaviour from others:

- How many of us would accept a medical doctor giving us a prescription for a banned drug, simply because he or she was three months behind in reading banned drug listings?
- How many of us are quite happy to repeat the same instruction umpteen times to cancel the milk or papers?
- We expect people to pass on telephone messages and feel annoyed when they forget.
- We expect people to return phone calls when they say they will.

No doubt we could fill a book on its own with examples of people just being sloppy. Examples that demonstrate a lack of self discipline.

Achieving a balance

A manager has to achieve a balance between monitoring and controlling staff and relying on their self discipline. This balance is not just about 'style' it is also about:

- the job output levels demanded
- the ability of staff to exercise self discipline
- the willingness of staff to exercise self discipline.

Where output levels demanded increase so does the need, at least initially, for monitoring and control.

Where jobs change and new knowledge and skills need to be learned, closer supervision for a period is only sensible.

Exercising judgement

It is a myth that all staff want 'space' to 'manage themselves'. Some just do not want the responsibility. They genuinely welcome and need close supervision.

Deciding how much 'space' to give staff is a question of judgement. Increasing 'space' is placing a greater reliance on self discipline. Reducing 'space' is placing a greater reliance on monitoring and control. In our everyday life we take these decisions, for example:

- Having shown a teen-aged child how to use an electric drill we may well rely on him or her to use it sensibly without close supervision. However we may well decide to closely monitor and control the same teenager's completion of homework.

- We would not leave a very young child in a room with an open fire but we may well be comfortable to do so if the child was secure in a play pen. The play pen in effect exercising 'control'.

At work we have to exercise our judgement similarly. We should not give everyone the same amount of space in all circumstances.

Failing to delegate
Limiting 'space' should not be used as an excuse for failing to delegate properly. How often do we hear managers complain, 'I have to check everything myself because they cannot be trusted to do what I tell them'. This suggests the manager does not know how to delegate. He or she is failing to:

- explain requirements clearly

- provide adequate training and coaching

- provide adequate supervision.

Abdicating responsibility
Equally granting 'space' that results in poor supervision should not be confused with some vague reference to 'management style'. Often the expression, 'I let my people get on with their jobs without hindrance' is an excuse for inadequate performance management activity. It is abdication of responsibility not delegation.

Case studies

Jill designs an incentive scheme
The network director is generally pleased with the efficiency improvements he is witnessing in the branches. Bert's branch is the exception. A recent visit has revealed that Bert and his team are failing to monitor and control the activities of staff.

Despite the fact that efficiency improvements are still the priority, the network director announces he is keen to improve sales productivity. He has asked Jill to help develop an incentive scheme for the branch managers.

After a brief discussion the network director decides the incentive scheme should:

- Involve all the branch managers
- Exclude all other staff
- Reward the best sales performance
- Run for the rest of the year.

The winner will be given a one week skiing holiday for two. Jill works with network director to design the rules of the scheme and an external company produces some glossy brochures. Jill is concerned that:

- The incentive scheme does not reward all staff.
- The branches have barely finished basic, job related training. The introduction of this incentive scheme may deflect them from this basic priority.
- The prize may not appeal to everyone.
- Jim is performing better than all the rest and will probably win, so it is not really a very good competition.

Jim is not motivated by the incentive scheme

Jim is very pleased with the progress he is seeing in all areas of the branch operation. Staff wastage rates are falling as staff more clearly understand what is required of them. The staff are being trained and supported to meet their job requirements. Always a bit of a stickler for checking, Jim is learning to delegate monitoring and control responsibility to his own line management.

Jim learned about the difference between internal and external motivation on his recent training course. This has resulted in his thinking about how he can use his recognition budget to best effect. He knows his assistant managers very well and has some thoughts about how he might recognise the best performer among them. He knows the other staff less well. Therefore at a recent meeting he asked his line management to think about good performers and how they might be recognised. They have a week to get back to him with their views.

The internal post arrives and Jim reads about the incentive scheme for branch managers. Whilst he is confident he can win the prize he has no intention of going skiing even if he does win. Jim does not feel any more enthusiastic about his job because of the incentive. Indeed he is concerned that his staff will feel excluded. For the time being he will keep the brochure in the draw of his desk. The incentive scheme is due to be discussed at the next branch managers' meeting.

Bert reacts to the incentive
Monitoring and control is now being exercised by Bert's assistant managers. He is pleased that his assistant managers are so self disciplined. It means he needs to do very little to monitor and control their activity.

The incentive brochure raised Bert's spirits initially. However, a comparison of his recent sales results with Jim's quickly dampened this initial enthusiasm. Bert knows his branch is performing relatively poorly. He is aware that league tables are going to be published and the whole world is going to know he is bottom. This cannot be allowed to happen. Bert quickly decides to spend the whole of his recognition budget on a sales incentive scheme for his staff. The prize he selects is an all expenses paid week end in a five star hotel for two.

Case studies - Commentary

Jill's concerns about the incentive scheme introduced for branch managers are entirely valid. The network director has designed a scheme that does not:

- give everyone the same chance of winning

- involve all staff

- recognise the priority business need

- offer flexibility in choice of prize.

The incentive scheme has also been introduced poorly and staff were not consulted in advance. Basically the network director's crude attempt at motivating the branch managers will fail. He will demotivate and alienate rather than motivate.

Jim is unmoved by the incentive scheme and will hopefully continue to pursue his plans to use his recognition budget cost effectively.

Bert is being driven by the 'self preservation' motive rather than any desire to compete. League tables often have this effect on those who appear at the bottom. The vast majority of staff are comfortable appearing in mid table unless they have a realistic chance of winning. However, their behaviour will rapidly change if they suddenly appear at the bottom.

Bert's incentive scheme is as poorly thought through as that of the network director's. It is a knee-jerk reaction. An attempt to cure an unidentified ill with an external motivation technique.

Points to consider

1. Think about your job. Identify three tasks that others always need to remind you to complete. How could you become more self disciplined in these areas?

2. Do you prefer competing for a known incentive or receiving unexpected recognition?

3. Would you like your job performance to be compared with others and published in a league table? Think about your reasons for your answer.

- 6 -
Understanding and managing habit – Step five

At this stage in the 'seven steps' process we have:

- Ensured the job requirements are clear -step one.

- Provided adequate training and coaching -step two.

- Addressed any attitude problems -step three.

- Produced a supportive working environment -step four.

If the performance problem subsists we need to explore 'habit'.

Defining habit

Habit can be a major problem when seeking to introduce change. Habit is defined as:

- 'an unconscious behaviour'

By definition therefore 'habit' is not something we consciously think about. Over time most of us become aware of our habits because others tell us about them. They tend to point out in particular our habits that irritate most. However this tends to happen less at work, particularly if it is the ' boss ' with the irritating habit. Confronting habit can be an uncomfortable experience for both the person pointing out the problem and the individual receiving the criticism.

Changing habits involves criticism
A prerequisite is for all involved to understand how to give and how to receive criticism. This is explained later in the chapter. The definition of habit should then be explained and some non threatening everyday examples given.

Examples
Few of us consciously think about:

- tying up shoelaces

- putting on a tie

- buttoning up a shirt or coat

- brushing our teeth.

It's not long before driving a car becomes second nature. The examples are legion. If we had to consciously think about every one of our daily behaviours we would probably be exhausted by lunch time! It should be emphasised therefore that habits are not only natural they are essential.

Habits can be positive or negative
In a discussion on performance it should also be explained that some of our habits are very positive. They help us to do our jobs well.

Examples
Some of the individual's positive habits should be cited:

- always arriving for work early

- always producing neat work

- greeting customers by name and with a smile

- finishing a job before going home.

These habitual behaviours need to be recognised and reinforced. Often staff are surprised when they are told these things because they are not consciously adopting these behaviours, they are 'natural'.

At this stage the manager should have prepared the individual to discuss any behaviours that are working against job requirements. Often folk will have had some of these unhelpful habits pointed out more brutally by a partner, a parent or a friend. This is because many of our behaviours at home are repeated at work.

Defining criticism

Criticism is defined as:

- 'a reasoned judgement'

The emphasis is on the word *'reasoned'*.

The definition and purpose of criticism must be understood by all parties at the outset of a working relationship. This is because it is almost impossible for a manager to intervene in a matter, or confront non performance without appearing critical.

Successful teams
The most successful teams are those in which the individuals genuinely understand

how to give and how to receive criticism. They develop a mutual trust and understanding. They recognise that criticism is solely intended to help. They also accept that anyone who is prepared to offer criticism must also be prepared to accept it. The least successful teams are those that avoid confrontation at all costs. Avoiding confrontation may feel comfortable but the team does not develop.

Reacting to criticism

Does knowing the definition mean people at work willingly accept criticism? On its own, no. The reasons for this are perfectly understandable if we consider the power of the self preservation motive in all of us.

When we are criticised someone is telling us there is something wrong with us or something is wrong with what we have done. We will inevitably perceive criticism as an attack. If we are aggressive by nature we will argue and fight back. If we are timid we will keep quiet but try and get away. In everyday life we encounter criticism:

- When was the last time the driver of another car 'hooted' at you? How did you react?

- When was the last time you offered a loved one criticism or they you? What happened ?

- How many times have you been criticised and heard yourself blaming everything and everyone else?

When we are being criticised we rarely sit down calmly and analyse the problem. Often the conversation escalates into an irrational shouting match or a week of silence.

Responding to criticism

At this stage we need to return to the definition of criticism. To meet the definition a criticism must be supported by evidence. It must be *reasoned*. Remarks with no foundation that are intended simply to wound the receiver, or to score a point do not meet the definition. But how does the receiver know on first listening to the remark whether it can be substantiated? The answer is he or she does not.

The receiver has a choice at this stage. Either the comment is simply rejected or the receiver seeks clarification. In seeking clarification the receiver may well want to register the fact that the 'way' the criticism was given was unacceptable. A form of words that achieves both aims is:

- 'I have to tell you I did not like what you just said or the way you said it. However, it could be you have a point. Tell me; what evidence do you have to support your remark? Give me examples.'

If the person is genuine they will be aware that the 'way' they spoke was not acceptable. They should note this for future reference. However they will be able to offer evidence from which the receiver could learn. If the person was not offering genuine criticism then the conversation will rapidly close.

Learning to accept criticism

The manager
Managers have to learn to deal with criticism in a calm and controlled fashion. They will fail more often than they succeed initially. This is natural.

The staff
Staff will be influenced by the manager's reaction to criticism. If the manager rants and raves when he or she is criticised staff will view criticism as unhelpful.

Most managers can recall reacting to criticism poorly. We have all been over defensive at times. Some will claim that however irritated they are about criticism they never reveal this to their staff. Frankly this is a highly unlikely situation. Line managers may believe they achieve this but staff can read the emotions of their boss far better than the boss ever realises.

Reacting to criticism in an uncontrolled fashion
Figure 1 is a simple flow chart that depicts what happens when a manager responds to criticism from 'above' in a human fashion. The process is as follows:

- The 'number one' motive in all of us, self preservation, is under attack.

- The attitude of the team is adversely affected.

- The criticism is rejected out of hand, for example, 'Head Office people ought to come out into the real world, not sit in ivory towers firing off memos.'

- Instead of considering the criticism, all energies are devoted to making sure the team does not get 'caught out again.'

Most managers can easily recall instances when they have responded to criticism in this uncontrolled fashion

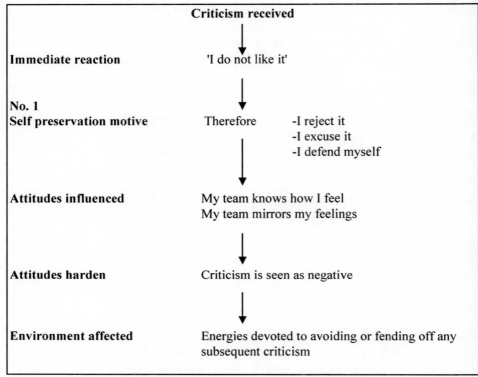

Criticism received

↓

Immediate reaction	'I do not like it'

↓

No. 1
Self preservation motive
	Therefore -I reject it
	                    -I excuse it
	                    -I defend myself

↓

Attitudes influenced	My team knows how I feel My team mirrors my feelings

↓

Attitudes harden	Criticism is seen as negative

↓

Environment affected	Energies devoted to avoiding or fending off any subsequent criticism

Figure 1. Uncontrolled reaction to criticism

Reacting to criticism in a controlled fashion

Figure 2 is a flowchart depicting how managers should react to criticism. The initial reaction to the criticism is the same. None of us likes criticism. We cannot stop this first reaction. However the good manager 'counts to ten' and asks the question:

• 'Is the criticism valid?' That is, 'does it apply to me?'

Remember we are still working to the definition, a *reasoned* judgement.

Example

A manager is responsible for one hundred branches. He or she knows a problem exists in the branch network. The specific branches have not yet been identified. If the matter is urgent he or she may well issue a written criticism to all branches. Whilst recognising the criticism will not apply to all, he or she is relying on local managers to respond to the criticism in a controlled fashion. To establish whether the criticism is valid in their branch.

Accepting criticism

If the criticism is valid managers must not only accept the criticism, they must also demonstrate to their teams that they accept the criticism. This has two benefits:

1. Firstly, the team's attitude will be right. The staff will willingly help to address the criticism.

2. Secondly, when managers have to offer criticism of members of their own teams they can refer back to the occasion when they were criticised. Remind staff how they responded. They will have set an example.

To become a really effective performance manager, a manager must engender an attitude in all staff that criticism is helpful. It is necessary and part of everyday life. Setting a good example by responding to criticism from others in a controlled fashion, is the manager's main weapon in achieving this attitude in others.

Achieving a balance

Offering criticism should, wherever possible, be balanced with the giving of praise. However, the balance must be genuine. Staff respond to sincere and consistent behaviour. The notion that we should always balance a criticism with praise leads to contrived behaviour. This is very quickly sensed by staff. It is much better to offer criticism genuinely and delay the giving of praise until it is justified. The key is for the manager to understand the need for 'balance' and avoid the extremes. Always giving praise, however shallow, does not motivate people. However, always offering criticism will demotivate people.

Managers managing themselves

'Step five' is not only about managers addressing the effects of habit on the performance of subordinate staff. Managers also need help to recognise and control their own habits.

When staff are newly appointed to supervisory or management roles they tend to view the role as 'doing things to other people.' Whilst this is of course true, it is not the starting point. The starting point is 'managers managing themselves.' They can achieve this with the help of their line managers and their staff.

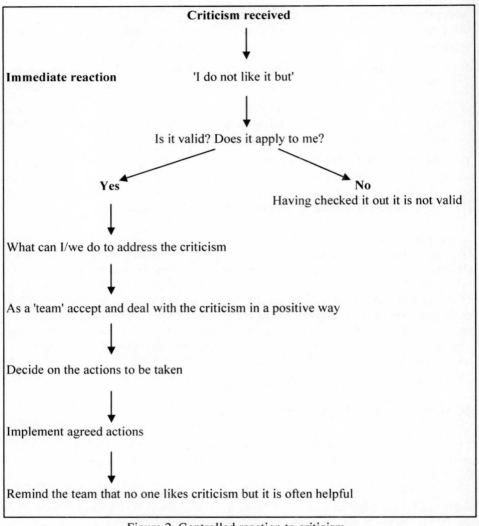

Figure 2. Controlled reaction to criticism

Once managers are managing themselves they will be far more effective. They need to learn to manage:

- themselves
- their staff

- their teams

- their business.

Even experienced managers need to be encouraged to manage 'themselves'.

Understanding ourselves

Most of us like to think we are people who:

- are fair

- hold balanced views

- listen

- do not assume

- avoid snap judgements, etc.

The reality is that in most of our waking life we do not behave in this way. Whilst perfectly natural, we tend to behave in a way that confirms our view of the world. For example, a person's appearance can lead us to sum up their whole personality in a split second.

We are all a complex mixture of:

- strengths and limitations

- attitudes

- habits

- prejudices

- internal drives - 'internal motivation'.

This 'mixture' will help us achieve what we want to achieve in some circumstances. In others the 'mixture' will work against us. The aim of 'managers managing themselves' is:

- 'To recognise and control their behaviour in circumstances where not to do so would work against them'.

Seeking feedback

'Managers managing themselves' does not mean their sitting in a darkened room and analysing themselves. A healthy degree of self criticism is helpful but, on its own, it is not the answer. We all need the help of others to establish when our behaviours are productive and when they are not. This help can be provided by:

- Our line managers if we work closely together. It becomes more difficult if the relationship is physically remote.

- The staff that work for us.

The better source of input is the team that works for us. Indeed most managers would rather hear about a problem from their own staff than have it pointed out to them by their 'boss'.

Before seeking input it is vital that all parties involved understand how to give and how to receive criticism as explained earlier.

Inviting criticism

Unfortunately even if giving and receiving criticism is understood it is still very unlikely that a subordinate will initiate such a discussion. If managers want to improve the way they do their jobs they need to invite their staff to comment. Two questions that will help managers identify aspects of their own behaviour that adversely affect the job performances of their staff are:

- 'Is there anything I do that *hinders* you doing your job?'

- 'Is there anything more I could do to *help* you do your job?'

The first time a manager asks these questions he or she must:

- take a deep breath

- expect criticism

- avoid interrupting

- truly listen.

The temptation is to fend off the first criticism by:

- interrupting defensively - the self preservation motive in control

- explaining the person criticising does not have all the facts

- rationalising the criticism away

- changing absolutely nothing.

The author first asked these very questions over 20 years ago so he understands the temptation.

The questions intentionally concentrate on 'job' related issues. They avoid inviting personal remarks. Responses managers receive will be many and varied, for example:

- 'You need to be more available to meet customers in line with your time-plan.'

- 'You do not complete the training sessions as promised.'

- 'You leave junior staff to deal with difficult customers.'

- 'You could sign the post earlier so I do not have to rush around at the last minute'.

- 'You could tell us more about the meetings you attend.'

- 'You forget to return phone calls. Customers then blame me because the think I have forgotten to tell you.'

Everyone else knows but you

A manager may well 'fear' asking the 'help and hinder' questions. We cannot control the influence of our self preservation motive. We need to recognise that these criticisms exist whether the questions are asked or not. This realisation can help overcome any apprehension. In many working environments problems exist and the manager is often the only person not to know about them. Once the questions are asked, issues can be identified. The manager can then do something positive to improve matters. This has to be better in the longer term than leaving disgruntled staff to mutter about issues amongst themselves. In this atmosphere the list of issues tends to get longer. The most trivial issues grow in perceived importance.

Handling responses to the questions

If you ask the questions you must do something with the answers. If you intend to do nothing do not ask the questions!

You may well feel swamped by the number of things raised by staff. Do not assume personal responsibility to cure all the ills.

Example

You have asked all your staff the questions and you have finished up with twenty issues. Proceed as follows:

- Categorise the issues into two groups. Those you need to deal with personally and those that the whole team needs to work on to find a solution.

- Address the issues that you need to deal with personally.

- Get your team to think about the other issues.

- Agree a date by which the team must come back to you with their solutions.

- Arrange a meeting to discuss and agree actions.

At the end of this exercise a couple of issues are likely to remain outstanding which no one can necessarily address, for example:

- 'You could help me by building a bigger staff room.'

- 'The lack of parking spaces is a hindrance.'

Because the majority of problems will have been addressed, the outstanding issues lose their perceived importance. The fact that their solution is outside anyone's control is recognised and accepted. Their existence does not detract from the benefits of completing the exercise.

Keeping to the job requirements
Remember to concentrate on the *job* you are asking your staff to carry out. Poor questioning can lead to responses that are not job related and this can be unhelpful.. It is useful when introducing the help and hinder questions to emphasise you are concerned with the individual meeting their *job requirements,* not whether you like each other.

Seeking positive feedback
Some managers like to balance the feedback they receive. They do this by establishing what they currently do that is helpful. Asking the question, 'what do I do that you feel helps you do your job?', achieves this balance.

Demotivating staff

In the last chapter we considered how managers and organisations seek to motivate staff. It is just as important to recognise the power of demotivating behaviour. It is illogical to devote time and money to incentives and other motivational devices, if this effort is more than offset by demotivating behaviour.

Asking the 'help and hinder' questions helps the manager identify demotivating factors and eradicate them. Often this can be more motivational than trying to positively motivate staff. We only have to listen to people talking about their working day to appreciate this fact:

- 'My company cannot organise anything.'

- 'My boss is absolutely hopeless and yet he thinks he is brilliant.'

- 'If I could find another job I would leave.'

- 'Nobody listens. I gave up trying to change things ages ago.'

Less often do we hear references to the effects of positive motivation:

- 'My company has introduced a fantastic incentive scheme.'

- 'My boss recognised my work today. I was really chuffed.'

- 'I received an unexpected bonus from my company this month. I was delighted.'

The 'help and hinder' questions should therefore be seen as a powerful means of motivating staff. Improving someone's working environment is motivational.

The vicious circle

The importance of managers managing themselves is best emphasised by explaining the 'vicious circle' to which we are all subject.

Example
The sales performance of a retail branch was comparatively poor. In giving reasons for this situation the manager stated:

- 'Most of my staff are married women and they have no interest in selling.'

The manager, at this stage, genuinely believed his explanation was valid; he had convinced himself.

The vicious circle starts and ends with the manager. In this case the manager had no appreciation of the 'seven steps'. Nor did he understand the importance of 'managers managing themselves'. Therefore at no time had he questioned his 'belief' that married women were uninterested in selling. This belief led him to make unconfirmed assumptions about the 'internal motivations' of married women:

- 'They do not want to be trained to do anything new.'

- 'They would be uncomfortable trying to sell.'

The assumption led the manager to behave in a way that inevitably confirmed his prejudice. His prejudice:

- Influenced the type of work he asked married women to undertake.

- Ensured the work did not include anything to do with selling.

- Resulted in his not providing any training or coaching in selling.

- Meant married women were unaware of sales performance statistics and knew little about the sales interview process.

- Inevitably ensured that the married women did not sell.

The manager observed the behaviour of his 'married women' staff and concluded his original assertion was correct. In glorious isolation the manager reinforced his view. From start to finish he had not asked one question of anybody!

His vicious circle looked like Figure 3.

At this stage the manager:

- Was made aware of the 'vicious circle' resulting from his prejudice.
- Received training in 'steps one to five' of the 'seven steps' process.
- Was asked to ascertain the real situation by interviewing each member of staff.

The outcome

Step one
He explained to his staff that their jobs included helping him achieve his sales targets. He described what they had to do to help.

Step two
He arranged for the staff to attend courses and on their return he provided on job training and coaching.

Step three
He explained the importance of the selling role. All staff were 'willing' to give it a try.

Step four
He provided encouragement, recognition and monitored and controlled each person's performance.

Step five
As time went by he regularly ensured staff did not drop back into old habits

After six months the sales performance of the branch improved considerably. With the same staff the manager was achieving his targets. The 'problem' did not rest with the staff. The problem was caused by the manager not recognising and controlling his own prejudices.

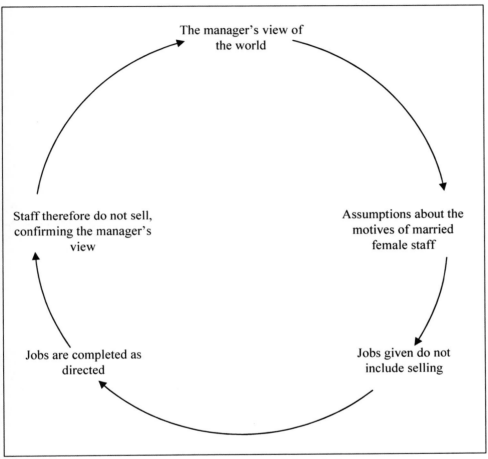

Figure 3. The manager's vicious circle

Treating staff objectively

In the example the manager put his prejudices to one side and learned a valuable lesson. Whether his prejudice changed fundamentally is not really the point. The point is that managers must be prepared to recognise and control their prejudices when at work. To keep an open mind. To ask questions and avoid assumptions.

Figure 4 is a diagram of the vicious circle template.

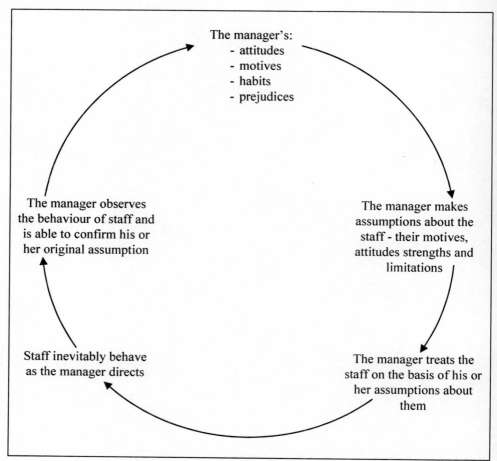

Figure 4. The vicious circle template

Developing genuine self confidence

Before moving on to 'step six' we need to consider the importance of self confidence. The most effective performance managers are self confident and encourage others to become the same. In such an environment the issues addressed in the next chapter are more readily understood and accepted.

The dictionary defines self confidence as:

- 'Having confidence in one's own powers, judgement, etc.'

Self confidence needs to be based on a realistic and open assessment of our strengths and limitations. Self confidence should not be confused with 'arrogance'. The former is a realistic acceptance of oneself, whilst the latter is an exaggerated opinion of oneself.

The benefits
Self confident people recognise they are not 'supermen' or 'superwomen'. They know and have accepted they cannot be good at everything. Self confident people tend to:

- enjoy their jobs
- perform well
- feel they are developing personally
- invite and accept help from others
- recognise and accept their strengths and limitations.
- avoid stress
- feel more in control.

Effective performance managers can and do create the environment that encourages staff to develop this self confidence

Case studies

Jill offers criticism
A recent audit of branch effectiveness by the network director has indicated that efficiency and productivity levels are improving. However the improvement is not consistent across all branches. Following discussions with an external agency Jill proposed the branch managers receive training in:

- understanding and managing habit
- giving and receiving criticism
- managing their own behaviour.

The network director agreed and chose to attend the course as well.

Jill was pleased when the network director returned from the course and asked her the 'help' and 'hinder' questions. She raised two issues and the network director accepted:

- He should have consulted Jill before introducing the incentive scheme for branch managers.

- He should keep her more fully informed about his views on the training needs of the branch managers.

When he first asked the 'hinder' question Jill noticed his expression became a little anxious. However he had avoided interrupting her and their discussion had been productive. They agreed to have regular, informal meetings to exchange views or criticisms. They both felt sufficiently self confident with this level of openness.

Jim learns to delegate

Jim found the training and follow up work in the branch extremely revealing. His assistant managers had welcomed all the new initiatives. They felt sufficiently comfortable to tell Jim that he needed to genuinely delegate. Jim did not realise he was tending to interrupt their work with unnecessary questions. The criticism encouraged Jim to think about his role. He recognised his job was to manage others, rather than complete tasks personally.

The assistant managers need Jim's help with supervising other staff and answering technical queries. They respect Jim, but they do not want him 'taking over' jobs himself when they seek his advice. Jim agrees they will have regular informal discussions about the 'help' and 'hinder' questions. He will arrange for other supervisory staff to receive the training so they can conduct the same process with their direct reports.

Bert dreads asking the questions

Bert could not claim he had enjoyed the recent training experience. He had always believed he was confident but now realised he was confusing social confidence with self confidence. Frankly he dreaded asking the 'help' and 'hinder' questions. He could still feel his cheeks burn when he thought about the vicious circle and how he so often falls into the trap described.

He had spoken to Jim and Jill about asking the 'help and hinder' questions. Both had tried to reassure him that they had got something useful out of the exercise. They explained they intended to repeat it on a regular basis.

In the end Bert spoke to the network director and discovered the network director had asked Jill the questions. Bert swallowed hard and met with his assistant managers on an individual basis. Their input highlighted a number of issues including:

- Bert's lack of technical knowledge and therefore inability to support others.

- His not confronting issues leading to staff demotivation.

- Lack of consultation before taking decisions.

- His abdicating rather than delegating authority.

In his heart Bert was not surprised by what they had to say. He had found himself defending his lack of technical knowledge but he knew he had done nothing to overcome this limitation. The recent sales incentive had gone all wrong and that was his fault.

Bert was beginning to wonder if he was cut out to be a branch manager.

Case studies - Commentary

The case studies demonstrate:

- 'If an organisation is seeking to become more efficient and more productive every member of staff has to change how they behave to a greater or lesser extent.'

For some, the changes required are seen as developments of their existing skills or aptitudes. The network director, Jill and Jim are developing as they practice new knowledge and skills. They are 'square pegs' in 'square holes'. Bert is beginning to conclude he is a 'round peg' in a 'square hole'. Interestingly if he had been asked the question earlier he would probably have answered he was a 'square peg'.

To assess a person's suitability for a role, a performance manager must exhaust 'steps one to five'. To reach a conclusion before this stage is premature. The conclusion will be based on assumption. It will also result, more often than not, in the individual strongly disagreeing with the decision.

When discussing motivation most managers think of doing something positive. Often it is more important to address issues and behaviours that are demotivating staff. Bert is managing to demotivate his staff. By asking the 'help and hinder' questions he has a chance to remedy the situation. If managers spent as much time on removing demotivators as they spend on motivating, most work forces would be happier.

Points to consider

1. If your boss was to ask you the 'help' and 'hinder' questions would you have

something to say to him or her? Do you think your boss knows you feel this way?

2. If you were to ask a member of your staff the 'help' and 'hinder' questions what do you think they would say? Do you feel happy to ask the questions at an early opportunity?

3. Consider the vicious circle and think about a couple of examples when you have fallen into the trap of assessing someone without asking any questions.

- 7 -
Assessing aptitudes – Step six

If completed properly, the previous 'five steps' will deal with the vast majority of performance problems a manager encounters:

- We will have ensured that staff understand job requirements - step one.

- Staff will have been trained and coached in the knowledge and skills necessary to do the job - step two.

- Staff will possess a positive attitude towards the job - step three.

- Staff will be working in an environment conducive to meeting job requirements - step four.

- Unhelpful habits will be recognised and controlled. Criticisms will be shared in a positive way. Managers will be managing their own behaviour - step five.

We have now reached the stage where we are dealing with someone who cannot do the job. They lack the necessary aptitudes.

Defining aptitudes

Aptitudes are potential abilities. Each of us comes into the world with a unique set of aptitudes. To develop aptitudes into abilities we need:

- opportunity

- training and coaching

- practice.

If we do not possess the basic aptitude we will not be able to develop the related ability into a personal strength.

Example
To consider this let us return to the average golfer. Most golfers can only dream about winning a major championship. They dream about walking off the 18th green having won the event by three clear strokes. Unfortunately most golfers come into the world with a limited aptitude to hit a golf ball. Despite doing all in their power over the years to improve, they remain average golfers.

The situation is very different with the golfing 'greats' such as Jack Nicklaus and Nick Faldo. They came into the world with an innate aptitude to hit a golf ball far exceeding most.

Somebody somewhere effectively took these talented people through the equivalent of the 'five steps' dealt with in previous chapters. This resulted in their developing their innate aptitudes into major abilities.

To ensure these abilities remain at their peak even the very best golfers rely on a coach throughout their careers to:

- keep their technique up to scratch - step two
- check out their swings - step four-monitoring and control and self discipline
- spot bad habits - step five.

We can reasonably assume successful golfers:

- know what their job is, step one
- possess a positive attitude, step three.

Assessing aptitude

Given the right opportunities we can all identify our strengths and our limitations. It is easier to try to complete tasks that call on our strengths rather than our limitations. With a great deal of effort our limitations can be good enough 'to get by'. However, we should not do a job that plays, in the main, to our limitations.

When organisations change, demands change and so do job requirements. People change less easily and less rapidly. Some people cannot change enough and the performance manager must help those affected confront this.

The expression 'cannot change enough' means:

- 'Individuals have demonstrated they do not possess enough of the basic aptitudes to take on the new job requirements.'

It is the responsibility of the organisation and its line management to thoroughly exhaust 'steps one to five' before arriving at such a conclusion.

Some people can 'change enough'. This means:

- They possess a number of aptitudes relevant to the new job.

- Their limitations can be 'managed' so that they are not a performance problem.

In cases where there are not enough strengths, or the limitations severely affect performance, the individual must move on. This decision benefits the individual and the organisation.

Example
A golfer has a golf handicap of fifteen. He has entered a competition that states all players must play golf to a maximum handicap of eighteen. In this instance he would be able to meet the demands.

If the demands changed and the maximum handicap requirement dropped to fourteen, the golfer may be able to develop sufficiently to meet the requirement by:

- devoting more time to practice

- employing a coach to spot faults in technique or to spot bad habits.

If the handicap limit continued to fall the average golfer would struggle to meet the requirement. If the maximum handicap allowance dropped to five, the average golfer would probably have to accept that he or she could not 'change enough' to meet the requirement.

Limitations do not develop into strengths
Once a limitation is clearly identified it is unfair to continue to try and turn it into a strength. Remember in this context a limitation is a fundamental lack of aptitude. 'If it aint in there it cannot be brought out'. If someone claims a limitation has been turned into a strength then they cannot be defining limitation as a 'fundamental lack of aptitude'.

Many of us can probably recall occasions where training has been used to try to achieve the unachievable:

Example
An individual, totally unsuited to the task, was sent on a second course on public speaking because the first course 'did not work'. He:

- hated the week

- saw his unsuitability recorded on video

- returned home thoroughly stressed

- vowed never to stand up in public.

The training was wasted and the individual was subjected to unnecessary stress.

Accepting the job is unsuitable

'Step six' is about enabling the person concerned to recognise and accept their unsuitability for a particular job. That he or she does not have enough strengths, or has too many limitations to make a success of the job. Refusing to recognise this situation means the person will work extremely hard, suffer considerable stress and still 'fail' . The inevitable outcome of this will be resignation or dismissal. These people need to be helped via steps 'one to six' to recognise this and take the decision for themselves to move on. 'Moving on' does not necessarily mean leaving the organisation. Often employees have valuable skills and experience that can be used in a different role.

Selecting the right option for the individual

There is a school of thought that states an organisation should not offer an individual an alternative role if it results in:

- a lower salary

- reduced status

- less responsibility.

The assumption is that the individual will be 'demotivated' and bitter. People who believe this do not really understand the complexity of internal motivation. Individuals have been known to select the option to remain with an organisation, on a lower salary or reduced status and still be highly motivated.

The key is the manager possessing the skill to help staff in this situation select the best option from those available. Rather than force an option on the member of staff, a manager can set out the options. If we assume an alternative role on the same terms and conditions does not exist, the options tend to be:

1. To leave the organisation under the terms of its voluntary redundancy scheme.

2. To accept a lesser role but remain within the organisation.

When exploring option 2, the manager should ask the individual what 'price' he or she is prepared to 'pay' to stay. This question explores the individual's motivation; how he or she 'ranks' a number of factors including:

- job security

- money

- status

- loyalty to the organisation

- ability to get an equivalent job elsewhere

- the redundancy package

- reduced responsibility.

If, for instance, 'status' is a very important personal motive to an individual, he or she will probably select to leave.

'Wanting' the job

People who really want to do a job for which they are unsuited need to be managed carefully. They will need a manager who is an empathetic and skilled performance manager if the process is to achieve a satisfactory conclusion. These cases are often much more difficult to manage than those involving people who just do not want to do the job anymore. This issue is dealt with in the next chapter.

Case studies

Jill discusses the problems Bert is experiencing

The network director has held his regular meetings with Jill as agreed. In these meetings they have discussed the training needs of branch managers. Jill is not surprised to learn that the network director has recently met with Bert as his branch remains one of the poorest performers. In addition there is a good deal of rumour around that his assistant managers are restless. The network director asks Jill to analyse whether he has completed 'steps one to five' satisfactorily. This Jill confirms. A further meeting is arranged between the network director , Jill and Bert and it is concluded that:

- Bert's strengths include, his:
  - social confidence
  - presentation skills
  - relationships with customers and third parties
  - ability to relate to peers.

- Bert's limitations include, his:
  - unwillingness to confront issues
  - inability to use the performance management training he has received as others have.

- Bert accepted the job of branch manager before the job had been defined properly. Frankly he would never have accepted the job if he had known it was going to involve so much staff management

The network director is aware that his company is about to take over a smaller company in the same business sector. He needs someone to work with their senior management and external customers to ensure a smooth take-over. Bert grasps this opportunity with both hands as it will play to his strengths. He will feel far more comfortable in such a role.

Jill decides all branch managers should receive training in dealing with performance issues that involve a lack of aptitude. She recognises these issues will inevitably arise as staff are expected to produce more.

Jim has developed a number of strengths

Jim welcomed the training. A number of latent aptitudes are now being developed into personal strengths.

The network director had stated that Jim was performing very well at their last performance review. Jim had developed as a performance manager to the point that his branch would be used in future to develop some of the best staff in the company. This recognition meant a great deal to Jim.

Jim is enjoying his role. Whilst he had always considered that branch manager was probably as far as he was likely to rise in the company, the network director had offered him another job. With the impending take over of another company, the network director wants Jim to integrate the two branch networks. Subsequently he would want Jim to be in charge of the branch network.

Bert is feeling much happier

Bert could only feel relief when he finished his meeting with the network director and Jill. He walked to his car with a feeling that a huge weight had been lifted from his shoulders. The new job sounded exciting but the main thing was that he had escaped from the branch manager role. Indeed as he drove home he reflected on the fact that he had not discussed salary, job title, etc.

Bert explained to people he met that he had been selected to help integrate a new company and this was why he was leaving his present job.

Case studies - Commentary

Jill will need to ensure that the network director defines Bert's new job accurately - 'step one'. This will take time because this new role will evolve over a number of weeks. However, the task must not be forgotten. It is very easy for someone in Bert's position to panic. To grab the first opportunity to escape from a role in which they are struggling only to find they are even less suited to the new role.

The network director should reflect on his responsibility for Bert finding himself in the position he did. Organisations must recognise they have a responsibility to select a person in the genuine belief that the person will succeed. Clearly it was the organisation's failure to articulate the branch manager's job requirements that resulted in Bert's appointment. Bert moved from a role in which he was considered a success to one which concentrated on his limitations rather than his strengths.

Jim has developed his latent aptitudes as a performance manager to the degree that he is being considered for a bigger role. Once again he will, over time, need be told more clearly what is required. He will then be able to come to an informed decision about the new role. Jim is clearly a successful and highly motivated branch manager. He should be given the option to return to this role if, later on, that is his decision.

Jill should consider how she can help the network director and others assess aptitude. There are many companies that now specialise in helping organisations define the aptitudes that are important in particular roles. Tests are then designed to assess staff and identify those who possess these aptitudes. Training and development programmes are then designed to prepare staff for new or bigger jobs. Whilst these techniques are by no means totally predictive, they can help. Clearly they cannot be used until an organisation is clear about the jobs it wants people to perform. They would not, therefore, have helped avoid the situation Bert found himself in when he became a branch manager.

Points to consider

1. Think about your strengths and limitations. How do you know what they are?

2. If you are responsible for promoting staff how do you assess their suitability?

3. Have ever left a job feeling you were not dealt with fairly? Identify where, in 'steps one to six', you believe you were dealt with unfairly.

- 8 -
Identfying internal motivation needs – Step seven

At this stage we are dealing with someone who has not improved despite our exhausting 'steps one to six'. The person:

- Understands the requirements of the job - step one.

- Has been successfully trained to undertake the job and is receiving regular coaching - step two.

- Accepts the job. There are no attitude problems - step three.

- Is working in an encouraging and supportive environment - step four.

- Has recognised and is controlling unhelpful habits - step five.

- Possesses the aptitudes to be successful - step six.

If we reach this stage we are dealing with a lack of internal motivation to do the job.

Defining internal motivation

There are many books on motivation theory, but in essence internal motivation is about our desires, wishes and drives. It is about what we 'want' at any one time.

Each person's internal motivation is:

- unique in its construction

- changes as circumstances change

- changes over time.

It is therefore a very complex area which often the individual does not explore or understand.

Exploring an individual's motivation

The performance manager needs to find a means of exploring an individual's internal motivation at work. The manager achieves this by asking questions that concentrate on the job's requirements. He or she finds out what the member of staff 'enjoys' doing and 'hates' doing.

By concentrating on the job the manager can identify what the individual:

- does enjoy
- did enjoy
- does not enjoy
- no longer enjoys
- has never enjoyed.

Remember, in this context the person is an unsatisfactory performer. His or her lack of internal motivation is causing performance problems.

Recognising internal motivation needs

The key is to get the individual to recognise that his or her internal motivation needs are not being satisfied. This can be because:

- The job has changed so dramatically that it would not be one they would now seek.
- Their own desires have changed over time. What satisfied them once no longer does.
- They accepted a job but did not really understand what it involved.

Confronting a lack of job motivation

There is a lot of truth in the saying:

- 'You can take a horse to water but you cannot make it drink.'

Often managers feel they should be able to motivate all staff. Frankly this goal is unrealistic. Managers responsibilities in the area of motivation are:

- To understand and practice positive external motivation techniques.
- To identify and remove demotivating factors.
- To recognise and accept the uniqueness of a person's internal motivation.

Once mangers understand the uniqueness of internal motivation they recognise the futility of trying to motivate everyone. People need to be 'thirsty' for the work they are required to do. If this does not exist the fact must be recognised and accepted by all parties. All parties includes the individual concerned who must accept that non performance is not an option. Either the job is completed entirely satisfactorily or the individual moves to another job, or leaves.

In considering these options the individual will be influenced by many considerations:

- 'I hate the job but where will I get another?'

- 'I need the money.'

- 'What about the family?'

- 'What will people think?'

At this stage the manager cannot choose the option for the individual, but he or she can help the individual look at the options as rationally as possible.

Option one - Move to another job or leave

The performance manager should help the individual consider this option by getting him or her to work through the following points:

- 'Are there any parts of your current job you actually enjoy? If there are write them down and explain why you enjoy them.'

- 'As honestly as you can, write down the parts of your job you do not enjoy and explain why.'

- 'What jobs, or parts of jobs, have you enjoyed in the past that no longer form part of your current role? Write them down. Would you still enjoy them today?'

- 'What do you enjoy doing outside work? Write these things down.'

- 'Ask your family and close friends to tell you what they think you seem to enjoy most.'

- 'If you could design your own job what would it look like?'

Establishing what people enjoy doing outside of work can provide useful information when looking at job options. For example, it is rare to find someone who is gregarious outside of work not wanting to be with people in work.

Option two- Remain in a job you do not want.

The performance manager should help the individual think through the following:

- 'As you do not naturally want to do the job you will have to be closely monitored and controlled to ensure you do it properly. How would you feel about that?'

- 'If close monitoring and control does not work your performance reports will reflect this. Formal disciplinary procedure will be invoked and disciplinary action taken. This could mean dismissal.'

- 'Your not enjoying your work will inevitably adversely affect your private life.'

Allowing time to reflect

Giving people time to reflect and collect their thoughts on these issues is vital if the optimum outcome is to be achieved. The manager, whilst being empathetic, must be totally honest. The individual must be helped to confront all issues, even if some of the issues appear unpleasant.

Using specialist support

Personnel specialists can help managers explore internal motivation needs with the use of various tests and questionnaires. If such a facility exists it should be used as it will help the *individual* reach the decision. If someone no longer wants a particular job it is much better if he or she reaches a decision about their future. Imposing decisions can generate unnecessary bitterness and stress.

The connection between aptitudes and internal motivation

It is quite common to find a person's 'aptitudes' and 'internal motivation' needs do not produce a perfect correlation. That is, we do not necessarily enjoy what we are capable of doing well.

Limited aptitude but strong internal motivation

We can all probably think of examples of people who try hard but rarely succeed:

- the golfer who will never play well enough to get a handicap

- the actor who will never appear on a stage

- the runner who will never win a race

- the footballer who will never be a professional.

These 'out of work' examples demonstrate:

- 'We can all enjoy doing things to the best of our ability even though we may not do them very well.'

- At work however others set the standards and targets we are expected to achieve. Doing things to the best of our ability may not be 'good enough'. Addressing issues arising from a lack of aptitude was dealt with in the last chapter.

Strong aptitude but limited internal motivation

These are the people that frustrate those of us with limited aptitude, but strong motivation. They are:

- The professional golfers who seem to waste their talent.

- The footballers who give up the game early.

At work these people frustrate the performance manager. When they eventually leave, the manager will often blame him or herself for 'failing'. This is why it is important for the performance manager to complete 'steps one to six' thoroughly and to understand the uniqueness of internal motivation. There is no 'failure' involved.

Aptitude and internal motivation levels correlate

In the workplace these are the people who achieve what they want and enjoy what they do. Historically many organisations developed a culture in which everyone was expected to be ambitious and striving for more. This a business nonsense and fails to respect the value of employees with limited career ambition. Many staff can enjoy mundane work over many years and produce high quality work. Now many organisations tier recruitment in an attempt to recruit 'aspiring chiefs' and 'willing workers'.

Case studies

Jill enjoys her role

Jill is highly motivated to continue in her current role. She has never bothered to analyse why. When a person's internal motivation needs or wants are being met at work, they are generally far too busy to devote time to self analysis.

Jill does however recognise that as the Personnel specialist she will need to help others confront internal motivation issues. She therefore attends and completes courses which will enable her to use various psychometric tests and questionnaires. These will help her help individuals explore their internal drives. It will help the individual determine whether these are being satisfied at work.

Jill sees more of Bert now that he is located in the same building. She observes that he is so much more relaxed and happy. How different from his appearance at his last branch managers' meeting.

Jim is thriving on challenge

Jim is now meeting his job objectives. He really enjoys his role and the performance management activities he now undertakes effectively. His staff are developing and he is beginning to feel he could take his newly developed skills into a bigger job. He feels he is ready to influence even more people. The success he has tasted and enjoyed seems to have rekindled his ambition.

The network director has, with Jill's help, done as thorough a job as he can to describe Jim's new role. Because it is a new role Jim recognises that the description is not as detailed as he would wish - 'step one'. However he determines to accept the job with the proviso that if he does not enjoy the new role he will be able to return to a branch management job.

Bert recognises his internal motivation needs

Bert's recent experiences have led him to carefully consider what he really wants from work. He accepted the branch management job because it carried a certain status in the company. He had always considered himself to be ambitious so it seemed a good decision. However he now recognises that he had very little desire to undertake many of the branch manager's responsibilities. He did not want:

- to be responsible for staff

- to confront performance management issues

- to work in a large team

- to be bothered with detail.

He has concluded that he wants a job that:

- enables him to work closely with his boss

- gets him noticed

- involves a lot of social contact

- provides a lot of variety.

He always saw himself as a 'leader' but now recognises he did not really understand what the word meant. He is now comfortable to accept he neither wants the role nor was he capable of meeting its requirements.

Case studies - Commentary

The case studies seek to emphasise the power of internal motivation as well as its complexity. As mentioned in an earlier chapter, a person's internal motivation is a mixture of:

- common motives, such as 'self preservation'
- unique and changeable personal motives.

Jill feels no need to analyse what it is about her job that satisfies her internal motivation. Most of us behave similarly when we are content.

Jim is 'feeling' differently as a result of his recent training, experience and success. His needs or wants are changing. His accepting a bigger and more challenging role is an example.

Bert has reviewed his internal motivation needs; perhaps for the first time. His recent experiences have led him to recognise and to accept his:

- personal strengths
- personal limitations
- potential - the aptitudes he can develop
- wants and needs - his internal motivation.

Bert will be far easier to manage now because he is well on the way to achieving genuine self confidence.

Points to consider

1. List five things you enjoy doing and five things you are very good at doing. Do they match?

2. Can you identify three things you used to enjoy doing and no longer enjoy? Can you identify why this is the case?

3. If you manage staff, have you ever sought to match your external motivation activities with the internal motivation needs of your staff?

- 9 -
Defining good performance

All the techniques in this book are concerned with helping a manager improve the performance of staff to achieve results. This section considers the question:

- 'What is a good performance?'

Defining good performance – the options

Is it:

- **Option one.** Achieving or exceeding all targets set.

- **Option two.** Managing resources to produce the best results possible.

- **Option three.** A combination of options one and two.

To example the points raised under each option, reference is made to a retail business. The company delivers its business through branches that are physically many miles apart.

Option one

This option is often seen as the most objective method of determining good performance and comparing retail outlets. It relies upon:

- A reliable and equitable method of apportioning targets across outlets.

- A facility to adjust targets at 'company level' if necessary.

- A facility to adjust targets at 'branch level' if necessary.

- The provision of regular and accurate management information.

Apportioning targets
The system of apportionment can be quite unscientific, for example, a debate around a table. In larger organisations the approach is more thorough and employs computer models. The models recognise a number of issues that will influence achievement, for example:

- staff numbers

- premises facilities

- customer base

- penetration of customer base

- potential customers

- size of existing business

- economic conditions

- propensity of customer base to buy particular products

- competitors.

When being set, or agreeing, targets the manager wants to believe he or she is being dealt with fairly. Given the importance of 'attitude', the organisation wants the same outcome.

A credible system of apportionment is particularly important if the organisation is demanding ever increasing productivity levels.

Adjusting targets

At company level
A company can use the start of year methodology to apportion the new target across its branches. A sudden, unforeseen change in the economy is a common reason for a company adjusting targets.

At branch level
Apportioning targets fairly generates a positive attitude in most staff. To sustain this the targets must continue to be considered fair. It makes little sense to spend a great deal of time on the initial apportionment if targets cannot be altered as the year progresses. Certain unforeseen events at branch level may well render targets unachievable and they should be altered. For example:

- The premises are deemed unsafe and the branch has to close for six months.

- Half the staff resign and it takes four months to provide replacements.

The original apportionment model included assumptions about the premises and staff resources. If extreme events result in these assumptions being wildly wrong, the targets should be changed.

Providing management information

An organisation relying on 'option one' must provide regular and accurate management information. Management information produced centrally keeps the manager informed about performance against target in a number of areas:

- sales volumes

- cost control

- error reports

- customer complaints

- inspection and audit.

Most managers in most organisations complain about the quality of management information:

- 'I am given a monthly target but I do not how I am doing until the following month.'

- 'The management information is unreliable. I spend all my time correcting it.'

- 'There are key pieces of information that I never receive.'

- 'I spend all my time keeping manual records because I do not trust our management information.'

Improving management information is a continuing task in most organisations.

Option one - disadvantages

Having described option one we need to answer the question, 'does achieving or exceeding all targets set, determine good performance?' Without some qualification the answer has to be 'no'. The most sophisticated apportionment methodology cannot address influences and issues such as:

- the quality of the staff resource.

- minor changes in local business conditions.

- good fortune - unexpected 'windfall' business.

- management behaviour, for example, getting results in an unacceptable way.

- achievement of non financial objectives.

The quality of the staff resource and its management is the biggest influence on performance not dealt with under option one.

Option two

This option is generally seen as highly subjective. Some people feel it is reliant on keeping the boss happy rather than any objective measurement of performance. The approach raises a number of questions:

- 'How does an appraiser define and measure 'best results possible'?'
- 'How can an organisation compare performances across a network of branches?'
- 'How can you design a reward system that is seen to be equitable?'
- 'How can you ensure appraisers assess performance in a consistent fashion?'

The problems with assessing performance on this basis alone, renders the option unacceptable. However this option is capable of addressing the shortcomings of *option one*. If neither *option one* nor *option two* can provide the definition independently can they do so if they are combined?

Option three

However imperfectly, most organisations employ option three when assessing good performance. Examples of this combination can be observed working well and working badly.

Most organisations can develop option one satisfactorily. Organisations with good performance managers can combine option two with option one to good effect.

Summary
To summarise where we are at this stage:

- The achievement of targets is a major determinant of good performance.
- The achievement of non financial objectives should be a major determinant of good performance.
- Targets must be apportioned as fairly and as scientifically as possible.
- Events that affect the business as a whole should be dealt with as they arise by adjusting targets set.
- Major local events should be dealt with as they arise by adjusting targets set
- The main, local variable that can influence good performance is staff quality and the quality of the line management.

Assessing the quality of staff and managers

How do we distinguish between good quality staff and poor quality staff? How do we identify a good or poor quality manager?

Defining 'quality'
One definition of 'quality' is:

- 'The essential attribute or distinguishing feature'.

If an appraiser is to distinguish between people who have 'failed' to achieve objectives there has to be clear justification. Intuitively managers reach these judgements. A good performance manager can support intuition with reason.

Example
Two members of staff have failed to meet their objectives. The good performance manager will able to address the questions:

- Did they meet the non financial requirements of their job? - step one.

- Do they explain job requirements clearly to their staff? - step one.

- Have both parties received the same levels of training and coaching? - step two.

- Do they train and coach their own staff well? - step two.

- Have both parties approached their job with a willing and open mind? - step three.

- Do they monitor and control their work well? - step four.

- Are they exercising self discipline? - step four.

- Do they recognise their unhelpful habits and control them? - step five.

- Do they ask the 'help and hinder' questions to remove demotivating factors? - step five.

- Can they both do the job? - step six.

- Do they both want the job? - step seven.

The 'seven steps' provides managers with a checklist of questions to help them distinguish between performances. They help provide an assessment of the person's overall performance. It is possible for an appraisee to meet financial targets but in an assessment of overall performance score poorly. The converse is also possible. Much of course depends on the organisation's culture.

Case studies

Jill links pay awards to the performance management system

Jill has been asked by the network director to look at linking annual pay reviews to her performance management system. To date managers have been given a 'pot' of money and granted pay increases on a rather subjective basis.

Jill has advised the network director that defining good performance or otherwise is quite a complex exercise. Much work needs to be done to ensure targets are apportioned fairly. Any system must be perceived as fair by staff. Jill is very aware that the current system, 'option two' described in the chapter, is considered unfair.

Jill believes it should be possible to introduce a more credible performance related pay system because:

- Job objectives and job requirements are clearly stated.

- Managers are becoming more proficient performance managers.

Jill has learned the lesson of introducing things inadequately. She decides to bring in outside expertise to help her design an end of year report form. The form will be based on 'options one and two' described in the chapter. Once this has been done she will arrange for the network director to 'pilot' the approach with the branch managers. If this is successful they can consider extending the process to all job grades.

Jim welcomes the introduction of some objectivity

The network director and Jill now involve Jim in the early stages of new projects. They have found operational management input helpful. Jim has always had misgivings about the subjective award of pay increases and is keen to help. He will prepare a set of guidelines to help appraisers exercise discretion when considering an overall grading. Jim will also help the Finance department design the target apportionment methodology.

Jim is comfortable that the network director and most of his colleagues will be able to work with a part objective/part subjective system. The key is to control the subjective element by issuing clear guidelines based on the 'seven steps'.

Bert agrees that subjective assessment is wrong

Bert benefited from his branch managerial experience. He has become a better listener and is now more questioning. He also believes the old subjective system of pay award was wrong. Mind you he did rather enjoy the power it gave him. Nowadays he breaks out in a cold sweat when he remembers how he used to have favourites and award them more money!

Bert agrees a combination of 'options one and two' is the optimum approach. He reminds Jill that he has three staff in a specialist department and she must ensure his needs are not overlooked. He does not want the company to concentrate solely on its staff in the branch network. Indeed Bert wants to be involved with the external consultants from the outset so he can contribute to the design of the system. This will help him to understand what is involved before he talks to his staff.

Case studies - Commentary

The case studies emphasise that managers must be skilled in performance management practice. The need becomes even greater if the organisation wants to link pay awards to assessments of good or poor performance.

Jill is right to conclude that performance related pay awards require careful introduction. The system and the documentation must be designed and introduced carefully.

Bert's feelings of embarrassment indicate he is thinking a good deal more than at the end of chapter one.

Points to consider

1. If you are granted pay increases linked to your performance, how is this done. Is the system:
   - inflexibly linked to outputs
   - too subjective
   - just about right?

2. There is a school of thought that believes linking performance related pay awards to a performance management system should be avoided. Do you agree? If 'yes', how would you justify performance related pay awards?

3. Most organisations no longer award salary increments each year based on service. Why do you think they moved away from this approach and adopted performance related pay award systems?

- 10 -
Debriefing skills

The 'seven steps' framework helps the performance manager analyse information. As with all diagnostic tools, the 'seven steps' relies on good quality information to reach an accurate diagnosis. The quality of the information depends on the willingness of staff to provide it and the interviewing skill of the manager to elicit it. We have covered 'managers managing themselves' and 'criticism' and these help engender willingness in staff to give information. This section deals with:

- The purpose, structure and style of a debriefing interview.

- The skills a manager needs to elicit information. These are debriefing skills.

Types of interview

There are many types of interview:

- job recruitment

- job selection

- performance appraisal

- job disciplinary

- debriefing

- sales

- counselling, etc.

Each has a specific purpose, structure and style and each requires particular skills of the interviewer.

Debriefing interviews

Purpose
A debriefing interview is a meeting between a performance manager and a member of staff to help achieve the performance manager's objective:

- 'To help someone help him or herself improve or develop performance.'

The debriefer must always remember the purpose of the exercise. Debriefing techniques are quite powerful and should not be used gratuitously. The purpose of a debriefing interview should be explained to the interviewee at the outset. The meeting is seeking to establish:

- 'How well you are meeting the requirements of your job.'

- 'How I can help you help yourself improve in areas not up to standard.'

- 'How I can help you develop your areas of strength.'

In subsequent debriefing interviews the debriefer should start the interview by stating:

- 'Let us review how well the action points from our last meeting have been completed.'

Sharing success
Debriefing interviews can also be used to identify what a person did to achieve a successful outcome. This can produce useful lessons for others. Therefore whilst the techniques are most commonly used to help address performance problems they can be used to analyse 'success' as well.

Structure
Interviewers should recognise the importance of:

Being brief
Debriefing interviews should be brief because they call for a good deal of concentration from both parties and can therefore be tiring.

Concentrating on the issues
It is very easy to allow the conversation in any interview to 'wander'. A debriefing interview should concentrate on a few selected issues.

Agreeing written action points
Each time an action point is agreed both parties should make a record. The form of words used should be clear and unambiguous.

Setting time-scales
Action points should include a time-scale. These must be realistic time-scales or they will be demotivating.

Conducting the interview in suitable surroundings

The debriefer should ensure the environment is:

- private

- comfortable

- relaxed.

It must be remembered that the debriefee will initially feel apprehensive. The debriefer wants an honest and open exchange of views and the physical surroundings can help achieve this.

Style
A debriefer needs to be in control of the interview ensuring:

- the conversation keeps to the point

- that success and failure are identified

- the interview is relatively brief.

To help achieve this aim the debriefer must explain the style of the interview at the outset. To achieve the optimum benefit the debriefer will:

- Follow a clear and logical sequence and concentrate on the facts.

- Possibly need to interrupt the interviewee on occasions.

Interruption
The debriefer should explain that interruption is a perfectly normal part of any debrief. The interviewee should not be concerned. For example, the debriefer may not ask a question clearly enough. This could lead to the interviewee not providing the required information. In such an instance the debriefer will interrupt the conversation and rephrase the question.

Because the interviews inevitably involve criticism they need to be conducted in an empathetic manner.

Influencing the debriefee's attitude

In chapter four we discussed the power of 'attitude'. We want the debriefee to approach the interview positively. Relating events within a person's everyday experience can help develop this positive attitude.

Example

Most of us have experienced an appointment with our doctor. The appointment is similar to a debriefing interview. A GP will listen to our description of symptoms and then ask us a series of questions seeking factual, honest answers:

- 'How much alcohol do you drink?'

- 'How many cigarettes do you smoke?'

- 'How much exercise do you take?'

- 'What is your weight?'

- 'What do you eat?'

It is upon our symptoms and answers that the GP will reach a diagnosis. Are we always totally honest with our GP? If we believe the GP will avoid being too judgemental then 'yes' because we want the appropriate treatment.

A manager can similarly be faced with 'symptoms' of a performance problem:

- poor sales figures

- absenteeism

- clerical errors.

The manager will need to ask questions to arrive at an accurate diagnosis and decide upon appropriate treatment. The 'patient' needs to be willing to help by answering questions honestly.

Exercising self control

Managers must strive to control their emotions. The style of the interview will become more confrontational and less productive if managers:

- demonstrate anger

- become impatient

- deliver criticism in a heavy handed fashion

- interrupt in the wrong way.

Managers must always bear in mind how they would like to be treated if they were the debriefee. If they can, unhelpful confrontation can be avoided. The relationship should be one of a non judgemental GP and patient. No one wants it to be one of a barrister and hostile witness.

Debriefing skills

These are the techniques the debriefing interviewer needs to develop.

Concentrating on actual events

Referring to the job requirements, the debriefer will want to concentrate on what has actually happened in a given period. Whilst the period of time is entirely flexible we are concentrating on *actual events*. This means most debriefing is a daily or weekly activity. The manager needs to 'strike whilst the iron is hot' and events are still clear in the mind of the interviewee.

Example

A salesman has failed to sell a particular product in several interviews with customers. To establish reasons for this the manager will want to know what actually went on in the interviews. The debrief should be completed as soon as the problem is identified. It is far more likely that actual events will be recalled if the events are 'hours old' rather than weeks or months. What the salesman *thinks* he or she normally does can be misleading.

Questioning assumptions

Debriefers need to be alert to expressions that suggest guesswork:

- 'I think'

- 'I believe'

- 'Possibly'

- 'Usually'

- 'Normally'.

When responses are introduced with these words the debriefer should interrupt the interviewee.

Example

In a debriefing interview a salesman states; '*I think* the customer already had a product like our own'. The debriefer must interject and ask the interviewee; 'do you *know* the customer has a product like our own? *What* was the product?'

As managers and staff complete more debriefing interviews the quality of the information elicited will improve. The debriefee learns what is required.

Challenging conclusions

A debriefer will on occasions be faced with a response based on an unsubstantiated conclusion:

- 'The customer had no need for the product.'

The debriefer must then explore the basis for the conclusion by asking:

- 'How do you know that?'

Again the debriefer must seek evidence of what was actually said in the customer interview.

Assessing self discipline

In an experienced debriefee it can often be a lack of self discipline that is the problem rather than a lack of knowledge and skill. The debriefer must seek to instil this self discipline.

Example

A salesman is just not presenting a product to customers with a need for the product. The debriefer should use the 'seven steps' to tackle the problem with the salesman as follows:

- 'Do you know that you should discuss the need for the product in your customer interviews?' - 'step one'.

- 'Do you know how to discuss the need for the product in your customer interviews?'- exploring 'step two'.

- 'Do you accept the product is a good product?'- exploring 'step three'.

- 'Is it fair to say only you can ensure the need for the product is discussed in your customer interviews?' - seeking agreement, 'step three'.

- 'How are you going to ensure you discuss the need for the product with customers in future?'- 'step four- self discipline'.

To encourage the salesman to exercise self discipline the debriefer may suggest the salesman uses a simple checklist. During interviews the salesman would tick the name of a product after it has been presented to customers. The checklist acts as a reminder and a physical record.

Following up action points

Debriefing interviews should result in improved performance. The second debriefing interview should follow up the first debriefing interview and so on. Simple action points should be agreed and noted. Debriefing interviews should be brief and deal with a few issues until these are resolved. Follow up should be the first thing discussed at subsequent interviews.

Asking clear questions and listening

Questions must be clear. If they are not the interviewee may well try and answer what he or she believes the debriefer is asking. By listening carefully the debriefer can correct any misunderstanding by interrupting. Interrupting is often more acceptable than asking 'Do you understand the question?', before the interviewee responds. This can appear to be patronising. In any event the debriefer can only be sure that the interviewee has understood the question by listening to the answer.

Summary

The qualities of an effective debriefing interview can be summarised as follows:

- The purpose of the interview is clearly defined.
- The structure and style of the interview is explained - particularly interruption.
- The interview concentrates on actual behaviour.
- Assumptions are questioned - 'I think', 'I believe', etc.
- Conclusions are challenged - ask the question, 'how do you know that?'
- The self discipline of the interviewee is examined.
- The debriefer questions carefully and listens.
- The debriefer controls the interview.

Case studies

Jill receives some staff complaints

Over recent weeks some interviewing staff have been contacting Jill. They have complained that their managers are not treating them properly. The staff feel they are being bullied. Jill recognises that those contacting her are failing to meet their sales targets, but not everyone in the same situation is complaining. Jill further discovers that the managers concerned feel equally pressurised by their bosses. All levels of staff seem to feel under pressure from 'the company' to achieve ever increasing sales targets.

Initially Jill is a little confused as everyone has received performance management training. However the 'seven steps' is a diagnostic tool and relies on the gathering of quality information. Once Jill identifies the probable problem she implements a review of the relevant managers' debriefing skills. If they are poor she will recommend debriefing skill training for all managers.

Jim agrees that training is needed

Jill has telephoned Jim with her concerns. Jim describes her call as 'timely'. He has just sorted out an argument between one of his assistant managers and a sales interviewer. Their conversation had degenerated into a shouting match.

Jim had calmed both parties down and asked them to start the conversation again. Jim would join them as an observer. The purpose of the meeting was to discuss the interviewer's sales performance in the five interviews conducted that day. Jim identified:

- That the assistant manager asked poor questions and did not listen well.

- The interviewee was trying to discuss anything other than what actually went on in the interviews.

Jim concludes Jill's suggestion that all line management receive training in debriefing techniques is entirely valid. Now that the company is expecting greater production levels from its interviewing staff the need is urgent.

The assistant manager subsequently explained to Jim that he found the 'seven steps' worked well when staff discussed their problems willingly and offered information. When staff were not so willing his patience quickly ran out. Jim decided the starting point was to train the assistant manager in debriefing technique.

Bert benefits from training in debriefing skills

Bert had never really challenged staff about under performance as he naturally avoids confrontation. However, he now has a small team that is required to meet quite stretching objectives. He knows he will have to confront problems and he is keen to learn any techniques that will help him.

Bert received the training in debriefing skills. He found that explaining and introducing the debriefing interview as he was taught made up for any lack of assertiveness. The questioning techniques worked and frankly everyone benefited as a result.

Bert tells his wife about the course and the techniques he has learned. He is a little surprised when she explains she has used similar techniques when talking to him for years!

Case studies - Commentary

The assistant manager's experience and Bert's experience raise important points.

People responsible for others will vary in terms of their natural inclination to confront issues. At one extreme there will be people whom others describe as aggressive; at the other there will be people considered by others to be timid. The debriefing techniques will help both 'extremes'. The techniques help managers gather quality information on performance issues in an acceptable 'way'.

The debriefing techniques are powerful. Jim will need to ensure that his assistant manager uses his newly learned skills with empathy. The assistant manager should not play the role of *barrister* with the sales interviewer without justification. This is an abuse of the role of a performance manager. Jim may well need to remind his assistant manager that:

- Performance management practice is about 'helping someone help him or herself improve or develop performance'.

- Debriefing techniques help gather quality information efficiently.

- Applying the 'seven steps' will produce a diagnosis.

- The assistant manager should treat his staff in the way he wants Jim to treat him.

Bert should not have been surprised by his wife's reaction to his description of the debriefing techniques. Most of us can probably recall the reactions of a partner or parent when we said we would be home by a certain time and we were late. Did we satisfactorily answer the question 'where have you been?' by responding; 'I got caught up with something'? Probably not! Debriefing is about discovering what *actually* happened. When people really want to know what actually happened they 'debrief' naturally. There is no doubt that some of the most vigorous debriefing occurs outside work.

Points to consider

1. If you are required to manage the performance of others, assess how well you introduce your questions?

2. Use the debriefing techniques with someone at work with whom you have a good relationship. Debrief a positive area to start with. That is, use the techniques to discover what the person actually did to achieve a successful outcome.

3. Think about the last time someone at home wanted you to give them factual responses to their questions. Were you a 'willing patient' or a 'hostile witness'? Did they assume the role of *friendly GP* or *barrister*?

- 11 -
Implementing changes successfully

Introducing change effectively is a challenge facing most organisations these days. Most changes require staff to alter their working practices. This chapter explains how an organisation introducing change can ensure staff behave differently as a result.

Initiating change

Most large organisations employ specialists to review the organisation's:

- business direction and strategy
- product range
- systems
- procedures, etc.

Specialists are expected to propose changes that will improve efficiency, effectiveness and therefore profit. Invariably these changes affect the jobs of operational management and its staff. If the changes are to be implemented successfully it is the practitioners who need to understand:

- why the changes are needed
- how the changes affect the jobs they complete
- how to implement the changes effectively.

Responding to change

Fundamental changes

Fundamental changes force people to change; there is no option.

Example

An organisation introduces computerisation into its branch network. Jobs fundamentally change. All involved are forced to come to terms with the change; there is no option. People cannot ignore:

- new terminals

- computer reports
- printers
- the removal of paper records.

They are forced to learn and adopt new practices. They cannot function on a day to day basis in the 'old way'.

Change that is not fundamental
Not every change is so fundamental.

Example
An organisation launches a new product and wonders why it is not an overnight success. The product designers discover:

- Helpful documents on 'best practice' gathering dust in the bottom draw of managers' desks.
- Expensively produced leaflets or brochures not being displayed as required.
- Training programmes have been poorly completed.
- Procedure manuals are being ignored.
- There exists a general lack of awareness of the existence of the product and its strategic importance.

The most common reasons for this state of affairs are:

- The organisation is introducing too many changes and its operational management is 'swamped'.
- Those expected to implement the change can continue to operate without adopting the change.
- The introduction of the change has not been properly managed.

Introducing change and the 'seven steps'

The 'seven steps' framework enables an organisation to complete the introduction of change effectively. To ensure the change is implemented. Applying the 'seven steps' ensures that desired, longer term behaviour becomes part of the way people carry out their jobs.

Implementation - the 'last 10%'

We will assume an organisation has developed a new product and has dealt with all the marketing implications. In the mind of the designer 90% of the work has been completed. All that is now required is for its branch network to deliver the product. The way the organisation manages the implementation of the change is vital. Often this final 10% is the most critical determinant of success or failure.

Communicating the change

The staff communication package needs to address the following:

Step three

Even staff who welcome change want to know why the product is being introduced. Reasons need to be given, for example:

- staying ahead of the competition

- matching the competition

- critical to the continued success of the organisation

- better for customers

- making best use of the organisation's technological lead.

Staff also want to know the features and benefits of the product. Often staff are also customers of their organisation. They buy the products and services, for example:

- a new financial service

- a new model of car

- household equipment.

If staff can see how they would benefit from buying the product, their attitude to selling the product to customers will be more positive.

This first stage in the communication process is critical and should not rely solely on the written word. Ideally the organisation should:

- Produce an attractive and convincing written briefing.

- Ensure all relevant staff read the briefing before meeting as a group with their line manager.

- Construct the meeting agenda so that staff can air any doubts or raise questions.

Because the line manager understands the definition of 'attitude' the meeting can concentrate on encouraging an open minded approach in the team. Remember attitudes are based on, *information, experience,* or *assumption.*

Information
The manager needs to concentrate on the information provided. Emphasising the attributes and benefits of the product.

Experience
The group needs to agree to discuss experience when the team actually has some.

Assumption
The manager should discourage staff making too many assumptions that are just not sensible at the launch stage.

Once the product has been launched 'attitudes' need to be checked out regularly as explained in chapter four.

Explaining requirements

Step one
The next stage in the process is to explain what is required of staff. In preparing to launch the product the organisation should have thought through the tasks that need to be carried out, for example:

- research the customer base to identify customers with a probable need for the product
- display promotional material
- maintain records of sales
- supply stationery
- complete awareness training for all staff
- complete sales technique training for interviewing staff
- produce new procedures
- produce a timetable.

The list can appear endless, but if this stage is completed poorly staff attitudes are adversely affected. How would you react if on the day the product was launched you had not received any brochures?

The product designer and the management expected to deliver the product should work together to prepare this stage of the process.

Completing the training

Step two
Having addressed 'steps three and one' staff need to be trained to carry out their new responsibilities.

Knowledge training
Technical knowledge about the terms of the product and the procedures to be followed should ideally be presented in a written, programmed learning format. This modular approach has three main benefits:

- Knowledge training can be tailored to suit different job requirements.

- The individual can 'self test' at the end of short sections.

- The individual can retain the document for revision purposes.

At the end of a set period managers can formally test their staff and address any shortcomings.

Skill training
Skill training requires interaction between the trainer and the trainee. The trainer should proceed as follows:

- Demonstrate the skill. Show how best to present the product in an interview.

- Get the trainee to practise the behaviour under supervision.

Before allowing a trainee to use new skills with a customer regular practice is vital. Most organisations employ 'role-play' techniques with the trainer or manager playing the part of the customer.

Prioritising training needs
In constructing a training programme for staff an organisation needs to decide to what extent 'must knows' need to be augmented by 'should and could' knows.

Example
A member of staff is required to issue leaflets on the new product to customers and make a note of the names of the customers.

'Must knows': The individual must know where the leaflets are kept and where to record the names of customers.

'Should and could knows': It may well help if the individual knows that the manager intends subsequently contacting these customers personally.

'Must knows' deal with what has to be done. 'Should and could' knows deal with 'why' the 'whats' need to be done. They give people a better understanding of the purpose of their job and its importance. The information helps maintain positive attitudes.

Creating the right environment

Step four
As explained in chapter five, 'step four' deals with:

- monitoring and control
- self discipline
- external motivation.

Because 'step one' has been dealt with thoroughly it is easier to determine what needs to be monitored and controlled and how best to monitor and control.

Monitoring and control and self discipline
In the example used above the manager can monitor and control the activities of staff by:

- Examining paper records regularly. These records will reveal the number of customers given a leaflet.
- Debriefing the individuals as necessary.
- Maintaining the importance of the job in the minds of staff by asking on a regular basis 'how things are going'. Responding as necessary.
- Using tests to monitor knowledge levels and role plays to assess skill levels.

These interventions help engender self discipline in staff.

External motivation
In the days that follow the launch of the new product external motivation will play an important role. It will encourage staff to get into the 'habit' of carrying out their new job responsibilities. Recognising successes and highlighting the importance of everyone's role helps achieve this. The product is seen as important.

Controlling the introduction of change

The process described above helps an organisation implement changes successfully as long as the changes are introduced in a controlled fashion. Benefits that can be derived from thorough implementation of changes can be lost if too many changes are introduced at one time. Someone, somewhere must be charged with turning the 'tap of change' on and off.

This will no doubt seem obvious. However, organisations have been known to introduce thorough implementation processes but then discard them because they wanted to introduce so much change. The product designer completes his or her part of the job, the 90% referred to above, but implementation in practice, the last 10%, is left to best endeavour. The net effect is the illusion of change being implemented effectively.

People are not computers

Modern technology means products and systems can be developed and changed with increasing ease. People change less quickly. If an organisation relies on people to implement change its introduction must be controlled. In many organisations fewer people actually deliver an organisation's business. This is often true despite the business becoming more complex. The ratio between the designers of change and those required to implement change needs to controlled.

Example

An organisation employs twenty people centrally to design and introduce change. However those charged with implementing change can only handle changes introduced by ten. It is better to employ ten people and be confident that implementation is thorough.

Often the converse situation applies. As the number of staff available to implement change decreases, the number of staff employed to introduce change increases.

Case studies

Jill has experienced introducing changes poorly

Jill learned very early on in this book that implementing change successfully is not just about telling people to 'cascade' ideas. The performance management system she designed had not worked because it had not been introduced properly. In a sense it was 'dumped' on a group of people who did not understand it or know what to do with it.

The network director's incentive scheme was another example of something introduced poorly and not implemented successfully. What could have been a good idea had now lost credibility.

Jill is being far more thoughtful about the introduction of performance related pay. The time spent getting the system right before it is introduced is well spent. It is a far more productive approach than wasting twice as much time later to patch up a poorly introduced change.

Jim understands the points being made
Jim has always thought head office tended to come up with some half baked ideas. Now he can articulate these thoughts more readily as all managers in the company talk a common language. Jim knows there are a number of 'head office initiatives' gathering dust in his office. He decides to box them up and send them back to the relevant head office department. He adds a note saying, 'if you want these things to mean something introduce them again, but properly next time.'

Bert sees both sides
Bert has received a box full of stuff from Jim. The box contains 'old' initiatives Bert had dreamt up and sent out to branches before he became a branch manager. Bert will be more thorough in the way he seeks to introduce changes in the future.

Bert admits that before he worked in a branch he genuinely did not appreciate the problems. He was complimented on so many good ideas and did not hear the complaints of those expected to make the ideas work in practice.

Case studies - Commentary

Most organisations employ enthusiastic people like Bert to come up with ideas to help others. Many do not fully recognise their responsibility to manage the successful implementation of those ideas. Involving those required to implement change at an early stage is vital.

Jim has behaved as any thinking manager should. Either the ideas 'gathering dust' are important or they are not. If they are not, the initiator should learn why. If they are, they need to be reintroduced thoroughly.

No organisation, logically, wants to devote resources to developing something new that does not work. Logic, though, is not always the first consideration. How often do people in large organisations pretend a new initiative has worked? How often will senior managers confirm something can be introduced effectively without adequate thought?

Much depends on an organisation's culture, but the answer to the questions will, more often than not, be, 'too often'.

Points to consider

1. Look around your place of work and find a file 'gathering dust'. Why are the contents of the file not used?

2. Have you ever sought to introduce something and found those intended to use and benefit from the initiative do not use it? Can you identify why this is the case?

3. If you are an initiator of new ideas have you ever been frustrated by people who fail to respond to your ideas as you would wish? Where is the problem?

- 12 -
Running staff meetings

There are as many types of meeting as there are types of interview. In the context of this book we are concerned with meetings intended to improve performance.

The purpose of a staff meeting

The purpose of a staff meeting is to help the manager meet his or her performance management objective:

- To help the staff help themselves improve or develop performance.

When managers bring groups of staff together they are taking those staff away from their jobs. A price is being paid. It is vital therefore that the time devoted to such meetings is utilised efficiently and effectively. The meeting should cover issues that could not adequately be dealt with in writing alone and where staff can benefit from listening to each other.

Structuring the meeting

Preparation
Inadequate preparation will result in poor meetings. We must ensure in advance of the meeting that:

- An agenda is issued. Its structure provides adequate time for discussion and attending to issues raised by staff.

- Staff receive pre meeting reading and are given sufficient time to read the material.

- Staff know the topics they will be asked to comment upon so they can prepare their thoughts.

- Staff are invited to raise any 'burning issues' in writing, in advance of the meeting.

- Charts or other visual aids are produced.

- Handouts are prepared.

- The number of people attending should be limited to approximately twelve. People more readily offer contributions in small groups.

- A suitable venue is selected. The physical surroundings should suit the style of the meeting, its duration and the numbers attending.

Follow up
The first item on the agenda should be 'follow up from the last meeting'. The meeting should review:

- Action points the manager undertook to complete.

- Action points the staff were asked to complete.

If action points have not been completed as agreed the reasons need to be explored. Fresh completion dates need to be agreed or the action point deleted. One way for a manager to affect the credibility of the meeting is to fail to undertake this follow up. This agenda item deals with the output of previous staff meetings and should be exhausted before moving on to the next agenda item.

Influencing attitudes
A staff meeting can be a very good vehicle for influencing attitudes. Attitudes are in the main influenced by *information* and *experience* and staff can share these in a meeting.

Example
A manager is concerned about an apparent change in attitude towards selling a particular product. The product was introduced successfully some months before but sales have dropped recently. One or two comments from staff suggest attitudes are less positive. The manager should:

- Explain his or her concerns.

- Encourage the staff to describe their attitudes towards the product.

- Identify why attitudes have changed.

- Encourage the sharing of positive and negative attitudes.

- Seek to influence the negative views with the positive experiences of others.

- Correct any misunderstandings by providing information.

- Assess the success of the meeting in influencing negative attitudes.

- Agree action points.

The action points will depend upon the manager's assessment of the success of the meeting, but could include:

- 'One to one' meetings with those who remain unconvinced.

- Agreement that everyone will present the product over the coming weeks and experiences will be discussed at the next meeting.

Because attitudes are so important the meeting must be structured to include this item regularly.

Demonstrating skills

Managers can often note a common lack of skill in a particular area. If we continue with the sales example above the manager may decide to:

- Demonstrate a particular interviewing technique personally.

- By prior arrangement, invite someone at the meeting to demonstrate their techniques.

- Structure the meeting to allow time for an expert to demonstrate the skill.

- Show a video tape.

Assessing skills

Some managers use staff meeting to assess skill levels. They use role-play and invite members of the meeting to participate. Criticism is offered. The main problem with role-play in a group setting is that most people do not like it. Unless the activity demonstrably meets the objective of a staff meeting it should not be used. Role-play as part of a more formalised training event is a separate issue.

Testing knowledge

Testing knowledge in a staff meeting is a technique intended to achieve two aims:

- To encourage staff to exercise self discipline. To accept responsibility for keeping their own technical knowledge up to date.

- To identify common misunderstandings or a general lack of knowledge.

Between meetings it is highly likely that staff will have received written information which they were expected to read, understand and remember:

- new instructions

- revised procedures

- new product details.

By regularly setting tests the manager is demonstrating that keeping knowledge up to date is important. The test can be structured in a number of ways:

- written test with one to one feedback subsequently

- team quizzes

- questioning individuals in the group setting.

Staff will be least comfortable with the last approach. This is because of the strength of the self preservation motive in all of us. The other approaches should be used unless the manager is specifically seeking to generate discomfort to engender self discipline.

Motivating staff
Used sparingly a staff meeting can be a useful forum to seek to motivate the group or individuals within the group.

Sales organisations view staff meetings as an opportunity to recognise success. An award is given to the best performer. This might be a bottle of wine for achieving a weekly or monthly target.

The structure of the meeting should allow for this activity at the end of the meeting. It is better if it is not listed as an agenda item and is unpredicted.

Brainstorming
This activity would not be a regular part of all staff meetings. It needs to be used when the manager genuinely wants to hear the ideas of his or her staff. It can encourage staff to own any solution reached. Brainstorming sessions are usually structured as follows:

- A problem or topic is explained.

- All those present are encouraged to offer ideas or solutions as they come to mind.

- The contributions are simply listed initially, usually on a flip chart.

- Subsequently each contribution is discussed and evaluated.

- An idea or solution is adopted.

Sham consultation
Some managers use brainstorming as a means of 'appearing' to consult their staff. The session finishes up with the idea or solution the manager wanted at the outset. This is unproductive as staff quickly recognise the game that is being played. The result is that they are less inclined to contribute when there is a genuine brainstorming need.

Addressing concerns
In preparing for the staff meeting the manager invited staff to raise any 'burning issues'. In structuring the meeting this item needs to be dealt with after item one, 'follow up'.

The reason for this is that if someone has a 'burning issue' it will be all they think about until it is dealt with. The manager should approach this item as follows:

- Announce that he or she has received and read the issues.

- List those 'common' issues that will be dealt with during the meeting.

- Describe any issues that have been dealt with in advance of the meeting.

- Describe any issues that are outstanding and explain how they will be addressed.

Staff rarely expect all issues raised to be answered immediately. They do expect the manager to treat their input seriously. As long as this happens staff will respect and value the process.

Reviewing performance

Many organisations expect staff to achieve individually set targets. A staff meeting will therefore often include an agenda item devoted to a review of performance. In structuring this part of the meeting the manager must:

- Remember the purpose of a staff meeting.

- Recognise staff meetings should augment, not replace 'one to one' reviews.

- Understand there is value in discussing success and failure if all can benefit.

Debriefing

In chapter 10 debriefing techniques were described. It is quite possible to use debriefing techniques in a staff meeting. The manager selects one individual and debriefs that individual in front of the group as a whole.

Debriefing a 'good' performance can provide others in the group with very practical ideas. Because the debriefee is successful the approach involves little risk.

Debriefing 'poor' performance in a staff meeting should normally be avoided. The reasons for this are:

- Debriefing poor performance inevitably involves criticism.

- The individual will feel uncomfortable.

- Others at the meeting will feel uncomfortable.

- Reasons for poor performance should already be known. They can be shared in a more comfortable manner.

- The manager's ability to debrief effectively and in an acceptable fashion is more than offset by how people feel when in groups.

Fundamentally managers debriefing poor performance in a group setting are employing 'discomfort' to achieve a goal. Where other techniques have failed this approach can be successful. It must however be used sparingly or it will be perceived as excessive use of 'a stick' to change behaviour. This is particularly true in cases where the line manager - subordinate relationship is not well established.

Supplying notes

Individuals making their own notes should be kept to a minimum. The reasons for this are:

- few people hearing a spoken message record it accurately

- time is wasted

- there is duplication of effort

- people when writing tend not to be listening.

There is very little point in staff having to make notes if they can be produced by one person, typed up and issued. This not only means staff are free to concentrate on discussions, it means they all receive the same record of the meeting.

Controlling the meeting

The person calling the meeting should direct and control the meeting. He or she should ensure:

- The agenda items are prioritised if all items cannot be covered in the time available.

- The meeting does not overrun its stated finishing time. The duration of the meeting should be prescribed at the outset. Overrunning a schedule is poor control and, if it is an evening meeting, counter productive. We can all recall attending such meetings and observing the reactions of attendees, for example, they:
    - keep looking at their watches
    - keep quiet to speed things up
    - 'look daggers' at anyone who asks a question.

- Breaks are taken if concentration levels are obviously waning.

- Everyone is involved.

- Visual aids are clear and can be read by all.

- Issues raised during the meeting are addressed in one of the following ways:

- at the time
- later in the meeting
- a note is made to respond outside the meeting.

- The style of the meeting recognises the maturity of the group. Maturity means the extent to which trust exists between members of the group, including the manager. The maturity of the group will determine the way in which issues are raised, discussed and confronted.

Staff are often required to attend meetings after the working day. To avoid fatigue or boredom the meeting must be brief, deal with a few points and involve everybody.

Staff will be attentive and look forward to meetings run in this way.

Assessing the effectiveness of meetings

Managers should regularly assess the quality of the meetings they run.

Overcoming habit
Running meetings can become an unproductive habit. Weekly meetings are held 'because they always have been'. They lose any real purpose and very few of the principles mentioned above are observed. They can degenerate into lectures, only no one is really listening. They fail to even please anybody; being seen as a chore delivering no benefits. Everyone feels the same but nothing is done to change the situation.

It can take a 'fresh pair of eyes' to identify that meetings are no longer productive because we are subject to the effects of 'habit'. Having said this it is possible to manage habit for ourselves to a certain extent by:

- Occasionally adding to the meeting agenda; 'How could our meetings be improved?'
- Issuing a questionnaire to staff.

Example
A questionnaire could ask staff to tick a box 'yes or no' against the following questions:

- *Agenda*. Did you receive the agenda in time to prepare for the meeting?
- *Agenda*. Is the number of items about right?
- *Pre-meeting papers.* Did you receive the pre-meeting papers in time?

- *Timing.* Was the time devoted to each session about right?

- *Duration.* Was the duration of the meeting about right?

- *Control.* Was the meeting adequately controlled? That is, we kept to the point whilst letting people contribute.

- *Presentation.* Were the visual aids and notes issued subsequent to the meeting clear?

- *Your involvement.* Did you feel you were involved in the meeting?

- *Follow up.* Did we follow up points outstanding from the last meeting adequately?

- *Queries/questions.* Were these dealt with adequately?

- *Preparation.* Do you feel we all prepare adequately for meetings?

- *Benefits.* Do you feel you learn something at each of our meetings?

The responses to these closed questions provide an overall picture and should be augmented by seeking written comments on possible improvements. Subsequently a meeting should be devoted to the subject of 'staff meetings'.

Case studies

Jill attends a staff meeting
A smaller company has been bought by Jill's employers. As part of a programme of familiarisation Jill is attending staff meetings in the company's branch network.

When Jill arrives the staff seem alert and friendly. The branch manager, though a little nervous, is soon at his ease when Jill explains she is simply there to educate herself.

The branch manager ushers everyone into a meeting room. He stands next to a flip chart with what seems to be armfuls of paper. He then proceeds to read from the papers he is holding. All the staff start to write down what he is saying. Jill cannot help but smile at what seems to be a farcical waste of time. Some staff have managed to keep up. Others are now completing their notes by copying those of the person sat next to them. Jill wonders why the branch manager did not simply give each person a copy of his notes.

The branch manager turns to his flip chart and reveals the first sheet. Jill cannot read what is written on it. Glancing around the room she notices all the staff are leaning forward in a vain attempt to see anything. Oddly the branch manager hardly refers to the flip chart and moves on to his next point. As the meeting continues Jill notes that nobody other than the manager has spoken. The staff, alert on her arrival, appear increasingly fatigued. The meeting closes and Jill cannot help but sense the staff are relieved and ready to go home.

Jim is now in charge of the branch network and Jill wonders if he has experienced staff meetings of a similar quality.

Jim describes his experiences
Jill speaks with Jim. As she surmised he is very much aware of the need to train his new branch managers in how to run staff meetings. Jim has attended three branch meetings and summarises his experiences:

- One branch manager issued an agenda at the meeting with over fifteen items. The meeting did not start until 5.30 pm. Six items were covered, most staff said nothing and no action points were agreed.

- At another branch the manager became embroiled in a heated discussion with one of his sales staff. Everyone else switched off.

- The last meeting he attended was simply boring. The manager swamped everyone with reams of paper. Whilst some staff were still trying to read the papers the manager explained what it all meant. Nobody was really listening.

- None of the managers knew how to use visual aids.

- None of the managers could describe the purpose of a staff meeting.

With regard to using visual aids Jim intends to seek Bert's help as he is a first class presenter.

Bert can structure meetings
Bert is delighted to get Jim's telephone call. He is very happy to help and looks forward to the opportunity of meeting all the branch managers of the new company.

Bert's current role includes responsibility for structuring meetings. He has attended a number of training events and has a lot of experience of arranging meetings.

Case studies - Commentary

The case studies highlight the need to train people to run staff meetings. Inexperienced supervisors or managers are often expected to conduct staff meetings without sound preparation. The training need is overlooked rather than ignored. The reasons for this situation include:

- The purpose of a staff meeting is not commonly defined.

- The structure of an effective staff meeting is not prescribed.

- The manager's performance is not observed.

- The managers running the meetings have received no training and believe they are performing satisfactorily.

- Staff are not invited to criticise the meetings they attend.

In the case studies the managers are being observed and their shortcomings identified. This will result in training being provided.

Well run staff meetings can be a useful tool in helping performance managers achieve their objectives. Poorly run meetings hinder the achievement of their objectives.

Points to consider

1. If you run staff meetings and want to assess their effectiveness ask your staff the questions listed in this chapter.

2. If you run staff meetings and do not know how to use visual aids to good effect, invite someone to show you.

3. If you attend staff meetings and find them tedious or unproductive analyse why this is the case. You will then be able to avoid the same pitfalls yourself.

- 13 -
Performance Management Practice in a business context

Previous chapters have described techniques that will help managers in any business manage staff more effectively. The techniques will improve any manager's *performance management practice*. The behaviour of managers is, however, influenced by a number of other factors. This chapter explains the relationship between performance management practice and these other factors. The relationship is summarised in the following equation:

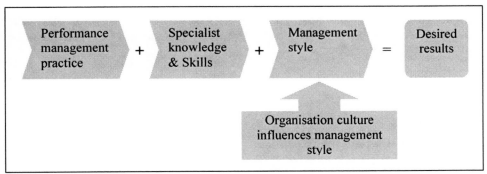

Figure 5. Performance management practice in context

Apart from performance management practice, two factors (inputs) in the above equation influence the achievement of the output, i.e. 'Desired Results', these are:

- Specialist knowledge and skills

- Management Style.

The power of an organisation's culture to influence management style is also recognised.

Specialist knowledge and skills

The basic 'tool box'

It is useful to view performance management practice techniques as the basic tools of any manager's trade. All managers of people should possess a sound understanding of the basic tools of their trade and be able to use them effectively. In their careers managers may well experience various business environments. If they understand performance management practice, they will take with them their general knowledge and skills about managing people.

Craftsmen and engineers will often move companies and take with them the tools of their trade. Managers of people do the same.

Adding specialist tools to the tool box

To be successful in their particular businesses, managers will need to add some specialist tools to the basic 'tool box'. The content of the job will determine the requirements. For example:

- Sales management.

- Production management.

- Quality control.

- Customer service management.

All managers of people are performance managers but not all managers of people are, for example, sales managers. Sales management knowledge and skills need to be added to a sound understanding of performance management practice, such as:

- Specific sales monitoring and control routines.

- Product attributes and benefits.

- Selling techniques.

- Setting interview/call targets.

At this stage the manager is fully equipped to manage people in his or her particular business or specialism. The toolbox contains all the tools needed to manage staff effectively.

Managers must now consider how they employ the tools to achieve their goals.

Management style

The simplest management style model assumes there are two extremes:

- Task centred managers (concerned with achieving tasks above all else)

- People centred managers (concerned for the well being of staff above all else)

Task Centred Managers
At the extreme, these are managers whose sole concern is the completion of tasks. They disregard the needs of staff.

Example
A manager decides to pursue a few short-term goals. This will require his or her staff to concentrate on selected tasks and increase their productivity levels. The manager selects the relevant tools from the toolbox to achieve this aim, but uses them in such a way that the needs of staff are ignored. Staff may well feel:

- Threatened

- Pressurised

- Over worked

- Undervalued.

The manager may well achieve his or her short-term goals but at what price? Concentrating on achieving the task and disregarding the needs of staff will, in the longer term, result in:

- Higher wastage rates as staff seek other jobs.

- Higher levels of absenteeism and sickness.

- Low morale and damage to the image of the company as staff moan outside work.

- Longer term goals being ignored and other objectives not being met.

People Centred managers
At the extreme, these are managers whose sole concern is meeting the needs and wants of staff. The managers lose sight of their business goals. Whilst everyone seems to get on well objectives are not achieved. Taking tough decisions and confronting issues is avoided. Staff become frustrated and lose respect for the manager. The manager ultimately loses his job, as do the staff as the business fails.

Management style is about balance

No manager can afford to adopt a management style that is permanently at either of these extremes. There needs to be a balance.

Pendulum

It can be useful to think of management style as a pendulum. It will swing to the left, people, or to the right, task, as the manager responds to particular situations.

Example

Managers may have to meet a crucial deadline. They will expect their staff to work harder or longer for a period. Their management style will swing to the right. Their priority is to achieve the task. Subsequently, to recognise the efforts of staff, managers may reward their staff in some way. Their management style will swing to the left. Managers should strive to achieve this balance at all times. Their predominant management style should be about balance.

Describing predominant management style

In this context 'predominant' means the management style that will be most frequently employed. Managers should describe this to their staff. In the main managers should adopt a predominant style that seeks to balance the often competing needs of task and people. This means their 'pendulum' will swing to the left and right in a consistent and predictable fashion. Managers can check that they are meeting their commitment by asking the 'help and hinder' questions on a regular basis.

Maintaining credibility

There will inevitably be occasions when the pendulum will rest in the task centred quadrant for a longer period than is usual. This is sometimes a business necessity. If managers explain why this is happening, staff will accept the situation. They will retain their trust in a manager's stated predominant style.

Adopting techniques explained in earlier chapters will also help managers maintain credibility:

- Inviting criticism.

- Asking the 'help and hinder' questions.

Communication

Explaining management style to staff will help them understand why managers' priorities inevitably vary from time to time. Using everyday analogies can help people understand how we all prioritise:

Priority - Task achievement

- Ensuring homework is completed before watching the television.

- Finishing the ironing although we are tired.

Priority - The needs of people

- Not having a bonfire on a sunny afternoon when the neighbours are in their garden,

- Not making a noise finishing a task if others have to get up early the next day.

We all have to balance our desire to complete tasks with an appreciation of the needs of people.

Management style and manner

Management style should not be confused with the way managers behave. Acceptable or unacceptable behaviour is sometimes confused with management style. This is quite wrong.

Some managers can appear to be 'caring' and be described as 'people centred'. In reality they may just want to avoid confronting issues. As mentioned above, they will often fail to meet the real needs of staff. Equally, aggressive personalities, described as 'task centred', will often fail to achieve tasks.

Developing management style

Managers can develop a balanced and effective management style by:

- Understanding what management style is about.

- Being clear about the objectives of their job.

- Understanding 'performance management practice' techniques.

- Developing their specialist knowledge and skills.

- Observing how others manage.

- Thinking about how they have been managed/are being managed.

- Understanding themselves (as explained in chapter 6).

- Involving their staff as explained above.

Summary

At this stage managers should be:

- Effective performance managers.

- Skilled in their own specialism.

- Able to balance the need to complete tasks with the needs of staff

We now need to consider the power of the organisation to influence a manager's predominant management style. Management style will be heavily influenced by the organisation's definition of success and failure,

Organisation culture

Organisation culture (what it is and how it develops and changes) is a very complex subject. It embodies the influences of many things, including:
- Company structure, e.g. 'plc'.

- The organisation's business sector and competition

- The content of jobs and their objectives.

- The organisation's commitment to staff training and development.

- Employment terms and conditions.

- The physical working environment.

- Social change.

- Legislation.

- Technology.

- Management behaviour.

Management behaviour
In this book we are concentrating on managers managing performance. Management behaviour is therefore the aspect of organisation culture considered here. An organisation's senior management, wittingly or unwittingly, influences how subordinate managers behave. This includes the 'way' they carry out the 'whats'. This in turn influences how staff feel they are managed. How staff feel they are managed on a day-to-day basis will influence their description of the organisation's culture.

The stated organisation culture
Organisations will often publish a set of values or standards that describe the culture they want to create. How they want people, their customers and staff, to view them and how they want their managers and staff to work together.

The perceived organisation culture
Ideally the perceived culture will mirror the stated culture. In reality this is rarely the case. In large hierarchical organisations, staff in different locations and different departments will have differing perceptions of an organisation's culture. The main reason for these variations is the behaviour of managers.

Influencing how managers operate

Formally
Organisations will often issue a list of values or aims to their managers. This is intended to influence the behaviour of their managers. For example, organisations may formally encourage their managers to:

- Adopt a balanced management style.

- Concentrate on all their job objectives.

- Train and develop staff.

- Balance short term and long term business needs.

- Openly express ideas, criticisms and concerns.

- Admit error or failure without fear of unfair treatment.

Informally
Whilst it is important for organisations to formally 'nail their colours to the mast', the exercise is somewhat academic if managers believe the reality is different.

In describing the culture of an organisation an individual will base his or her description on personal experience, information or assumption. Their attitudes are formed in the way described in chapter 4.

An organisation determines priorities, success criteria and invariably the predominant management style selected by its management. Managers will select the behaviours and techniques that will achieve the goals the organisation really values and rewards. They may:

- Adopt a totally task orientated management style

- Concentrate on the goals that are really valued by the organisation.

- Complete only that training that helps achieve short-term objectives.

- Never speak their minds.

- Blame others for failure.

Most organisations probably sit within these extremes, i.e., their formal expressions of culture more closely resembling the informal descriptions of managers and staff.

Stated and perceived cultures

An organisation that wants to limit the disparity between its stated and perceived cultures can help to do so by:

- Training and developing its managers to become effective performance managers.

- Introducing monitoring and control mechanisms.

Performance Management training

This book has been devoted to performance management practice. Managers who adopt the techniques described in previous chapters will know:

- How well they are managing themselves.

- How well they are managing their staff.

Problems will be identified at an early stage. Attitude and motivation issues will be addressed effectively. Communication will be open and frank. In this environment it is possible to identify disparities between stated and perceived culture. In a less open and trusting environment issues will not be identified and addressed. They will eventually extend the gap between stated and perceived culture.

Effective performance managers are able to identify specific training needs in areas that will further reduce the gap between stated and perceived culture, such as:

- Equal opportunities.

- Specialist knowledge and skills.

- Management style.

- Health and safety.

- Sex discrimination.

Staff attending courses need to return to an environment that will encourage behaviour change. Effective performance managers provide this environment. They ensure their own behaviour is appropriate and they influence the behaviour of others. Course attendance can influence attitudes and improve knowledge and skills. However, it is 'day-to-day' performance management that produces behaviour change. Changing the behaviour of people is a difficult and time consuming task but it is key in establishing a desired culture.

Monitoring and control

Many organisations have introduced mechanisms to monitor perceived culture, including:

- Staff attitude surveys.

- Customer attitude surveys.

- Confidential help desks.

- Grievance procedures.

- Personnel counsellors.

Information gathering of this type is fine if management behaviour changes as a result. This brings us back to performance management practice and managers managing themselves.

Managers conform or leave

Managers should seek to influence an organisation's stated or perceived culture if they feel it is unsatisfactory. However, many will feel the task is beyond them, or they have tried and failed. Managers are then faced with conforming or moving on.

Conforming

Most managers will adapt their management style and behaviour to accord with what they believe to be the real values of an organisation. They are able and willing to adapt because the benefits outweigh any disadvantages. They behave consistently and accept corporate responsibility for the way the organisation "does things'.

It is not unreasonable for an organisation to expect its managers to conform. After all it meets the salary bill. Organisations can help by defining jobs accurately as explained in Chapter 2. This includes organisations prescribing a particular job's level of influence.

Level of influence

In defining jobs, an organisation should reflect its management approach. If decisions are taken centrally everyone should understand this. Indicating otherwise raises expectations that will not be realised. This causes frustration as managers seek to influence matters outside their 'real' level of influence. The managers, in striving to meet a stated job responsibility, fail to conform!

Moving on

Some managers cannot or will not adapt. If they cannot influence the organisation's culture they need to move on. Their situation is dealt with under 'steps six and seven' explained in earlier chapters.

Summary

Achieving results through people is not, therefore, simply about performance management practice. It is about:

- Augmenting performance management practice with specialist knowledge and skills.

- Understanding and accepting what the organisation really wants.

- Adopting the management style necessary to achieve the desired results.

Returning to the equation appearing at the beginning of the chapter we can see this relationship:

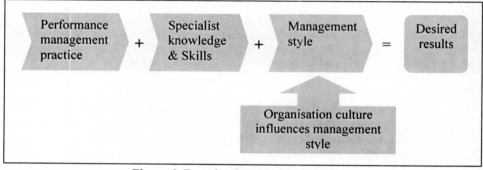

Figure 6. Equating inputs with outputs

The equation, at Figure 5 and 6, intentionally starts with performance management practice. This is the starting point. Most specialists start their careers as generalists. They subsequently concentrate on a specific aspect of their generalist work and become specialists. Accountants, solicitors and doctors are obvious examples. Managers of people are no different.

Once armed with all the tools of their trade, managers decide how best to use the tools to achieve results. They develop a management style in keeping with the organisation's culture.

The end result should be the achievement of those objectives important to the organisation.

Case studies

Jill highlights differences in management behaviour

Jill has recognised that managers in the company recently taken over, behave differently. Compared to managers she knows, they appear to be:

- Less open.

- Inclined to avoid confrontation.

- Less task centred.

- Lacking in urgency.

- Untrained in performance management practice.

- Lacking in specialist knowledge and skills.

Jill considers these issues in terms of the equation above. She concludes that the issues can be categorised using the equation. Some are to do with culture but others are clearly concerned with 'performance management practice'1 and "specialist knowledge and skills'. She has discussed the matter with Jim who is now responsible for these managers. They have highlighted a number of issues that need to be addressed if one culture is to be developed. Managers in the new company must:

- Understand how the company intends to operate; its stated culture.

- Receive performance management practice training.

- Receive specialist knowledge and skills training.

- Understand and be able to adopt a more balanced management style.

Jill recognises that you cannot start with 'management style". Initially people need to know how to manage. It is not a bit of good telling people to become more task centred if they do not know what the tasks are or how to get others to achieve them.

Articulating the company's culture will need to involve her boss and others. Jill recognises that the company's stated culture and perceived culture should ideally be the same thing. In reality, however, there will always be disparities because people are not machines. She will discuss with her boss how the company can identify any disparities. Staff attitude surveys and other mechanisms can help.

Jim is concentrating on training

Jim has already recognised the need to train his new managers in performance management practice. Specialist knowledge and skill training will come next.

He welcomes the 'equation' because it visually depicts the goals he and his senior management colleagues need to achieve. He agrees that the next senior management meeting should concentrate on the issues he and Jill have highlighted. Jill believes a weekend away will help everyone get into the right frame of mind. The environment must encourage open debate and 'brainstorming' if the meeting is to identify the actions that need to be taken.

Bert sees himself in the new managers

In helping to bring the two companies together Bert recognises the differences between the respective managements. Bert is aware of the work Jill and Jim have completed. He looks forward to the planned meeting. How differently he would have felt in the past.

In the new managers he sees the 'old' Bert. They all seem to get on well and appear superficially confident. Bert however now understands what self-confidence is really about and can see through their facade. Most of the new managers are really apprehensive. They fear the unknown and having to change. Bert understands their feelings He was once in the same position!

Case studies - Commentary

In the case studies we have seen that an organisation should state the culture it wishes to create. We have also seen that discrepancies between a stated culture and the perceived culture should be monitored and controlled. Above all an organisation influences its perceived culture by influencing its managers. This means concentrating on the areas described on the left of the equation. Producing managers who:

- Can practise performance management effectively.

- Possess the necessary specialist knowledge and skills.

- Can adopt a balanced management style.

Jim, Jill and the company's senior management want to produce a formal statement of the organisation's culture. They should, at this stage, avoid grand sounding statements that are not easily defined or delivered. If they concentrate on the bullet points above they will produce the management behaviour they want. Managers will begin to use a common language. They will be able to communicate with each other. They will breathe life into the words that express the desired culture by behaving similarly. For most employees, management behaviour is synonymous with organisation culture. If managers behave similarly an organisation is well on the way to establishing a common culture.

Points to consider

1. How would you describe your organisation's culture? How might it be different if all managers practised performance management as described in this book?

2. Have you ever left an organisation because you did not like its 'culture'? How important was management behaviour in your decision?

3. Consider your management style. Is it balanced?

- 14 -
A Case Study

Introduction

In this case study we return to Jim, 'the conscientious'. Jim is now responsible for the branch network of a company recently taken over. The company has:

- defined job objectives

- produced clear job contents

- introduced a performance management system.

The case study will demonstrate how the 'seven steps' and other techniques discussed in this book can be used in practice.

Questions and answers
As we work through the case study, questions and answers will be included at regular intervals. To get the most out of the case study it is suggested you answer the questions yourself before reading the answers.

The problem

One of Jim's branches is performing indifferently:

- Its sales results are comparatively poor.

- Staff morale is considered to be low.

- The branch manager is not thought to be a good motivator.

- Two members of staff have just tendered their resignations.

On the positive side the administration within the branch is deemed to be sound.

The branch
The premises are nicely decorated and there is ample space.

The staffing comprises:

- a branch manager

- an assistant manager
- a supervisor
- six clerical staff (mostly young and newly recruited).

Questions:

1. What should be Jim's first objective?

2. Whom does he need to speak to first?

3. Which 'step' should be addressed first?

4. How important is it for Jim to visit the branch?

Answers:

1. To gather as much quality information as he can as quickly as possible. To analyse the information using the 'seven steps' diagnostic framework.

2. The branch manager. The boss of any unit is the greatest influence on the performance of that unit.

3. 'Step one'.

4. Vital. Jim needs to see the manager in his own environment.

Gathering information

Categorising information
Jim is now familiar with the 'seven steps' framework. He understands it is possible to categorise information as it is gathered under the appropriate 'step'. Therefore whilst he always starts with 'step one', if he identifies information that is relevant to any of the other 'steps' he logs it accordingly.

It should be stressed that 'information gathering' is not reaching conclusions.

The first branch visit
When invited into the manager's office Jim noticed:

- The desk in the office was covered with computer reports.

- The shelves in the office were full of lever arch files, all neatly marked.

To have so many files 'to hand' is unusual. The manager must want the files to be so readily available.

Questions:

1. Under which steps should Jim log this first impression?

Answers:

1. Under steps six and one. Step six, does the manager like dealing with paper and maintaining records close to hand? Step one, does he see dealing with computer reports and maintaining files in his office as part of his job? These initial thoughts need to be checked out.

Exploring step one

Start with segments of the job

When exploring how a person sees their job, Jim seeks to identify those segments of the job the person feels at ease discussing. These tend to be areas of the job the person completes well and, usually, enjoys. At the very least it will be those areas of the job where the person spends most time.

The company, as mentioned above, has described jobs in detail. Jim has a copy of the document describing the branch manager's job. The branch manager's job is described under eight main headings:

- Managing and motivating staff
- Business Development
- Servicing Customers
- Judgement and Decisions
- Planning and Organisation
- Control and Administration
- Commitment and Energy
- Self Development.

Under each of the headings detailed tasks are listed.

It is easier to talk about the job at the segment level initially. If it seems that a problem exists in a particular segment the 'task expressions' can be discussed to identify the problem more specifically.

The first interview with the branch manager
In listening to the branch manager describe how he spent his time Jim noticed the manager appeared:

- Comfortable and fluent when explaining the tasks he undertook personally.

- At ease when talking about tasks that came under the segments; Planning and Organisation, Control and Administration and Judgement and Decisions.

- Far less comfortable when talking about his staff, his customers and his selling role.

- Committed and quite energetic in the pursuit of the parts of the job he considered important.

- Uncomfortable when discussing self development despite his having attended various training events.

Questions:

1. In which segments should Jim now concentrate his questioning?

2. What questioning techniques should Jim use?

Answers:

1. Those segments where the branch manager seems less comfortable.

2. Jim should use the debriefing techniques.

Isolating the problem areas
The branch manager's responses led Jim to ask more specific questions in the segments he concluded the branch manager appeared less comfortable, for example:

- 'tell me about your staff?'

- 'take me through the training plans for your staff?'

- 'describe your customers'

- 'how has your recent sales training course helped you?'

Jim followed up these opening questions with questions seeking specific examples.

At this stage of the information gathering exercise Jim categorised the branch manager's responses using the 'seven steps'.

Questions:

1. Jim's categorisation appears below but the relevant step has been omitted can you complete the categorisation?

    a. He possessed sound communication skills (step .....and step.....)

    b. He enjoyed technical tasks which he could undertake personally (step.....)

    c. He did not seem to enjoy selling personally (step .....) despite receiving the training (step.....) and recognising that selling personally was an important part of his job (step.....and step.....)

    d. He was very critical of his staff but there was no evidence of his adequately managing them. He did seem to recognise his responsibilities in this area (step.....), but that was about it. There was absolutely no evidence of activities described in the chapter 'Managers managing themselves' (step.....) Expressions such as, 'the staff are young and not as committed to doing a good job as in my day' were not supported by any evidence. It was a classic example of prejudice and the 'vicious circle' in operation (step.....)

    e. All evidence at this stage suggested he was methodical and reliable when dealing with detail and deadlines involving tasks rather than people (step.....)

Answers:

1. a. Step two and step six

   b. Step seven

   c. Step seven, step two. step one and step three.

   d. Step one, step five and step five

   e. Step six

Remember step six is concerned with aptitude and step seven is concerned with internal motivation.

Interviewing the management team

The first meeting had left Jim concerned about those segments of the branch manager's job concerned with people. If the manager was not addressing these segments who was? Jim decided to interview the assistant manager and the supervisor.

The assistant manager

The assistant manager was working in the same segments as the branch manager and seemed to hold similar views, attitudes and prejudices.

The supervisor

Jim then interviewed the supervisor who actually supervised very little. She was a form of 'reference library' for more junior staff. She did not see active supervision of others as part of her job role.

Reviewing the information

The branch lacked a performance manager

None of the senior staff seemed to be fulfilling the role of 'performance manager' adequately. Someone in the management team should be:

- explaining job requirements clearly (step one)

- providing training and coaching (step two)

- finding out what staff thought about their jobs (step three)

- providing encouragement and support (step four-external motivation)

- monitoring and controlling performance (step four-monitoring and control)

- instilling self discipline (step four-self discipline).

There was no evidence that:

- the management team was managing itself (chapter six)

- staff meetings were run properly (chapter twelve)

- there was any understanding of how to deliver and invite 'criticism' (chapter six)

- debriefing techniques' were understood (chapter ten).

Meeting the staff

Jim then met with each member of staff. He simply asked them to describe to him what it was like to work in the branch. This open question would reveal their attitudes, step three. Jim followed up this general question with others to help him address his preliminary assessment referred to above. Their input enabled Jim to confirm his assessment.

Taking action

At this stage Jim realised he had a lot of work to do with the branch management team. However this would take time and Jim was facing two resignations and staff without a performance manager. Something needed to be done in the short term.

Short term

Jim decided to bring someone into the branch, on a temporary basis, to address the valid and urgent needs of the staff. Someone strong in the 'people' segments of the branch management role. This person would hold things together whilst Jim worked with the branch manager. The staff welcomed this action. Those who had tendered resignations agreed to withdraw them for the time being.

Briefing the branch management team

Jim explained:

- That the staff had criticised the way the branch was managed.

- What he intended to do in the short term.

- What he wanted each of them to do over the next few weeks.

This resulted in the assistant manager accepting sole responsibility for tasks the management team had tended to share or duplicate. These tasks played to the assistant manager's strengths so that Jim could concentrate on the manager.

Questions:

1. Without mentioning any names Jim had relayed the feelings of staff to the branch management team. How do you think they reacted and why?

2. What should Jim do in response to their reactions?

Answers:

1. They reacted very defensively. Jim had expected this reaction as he was offering 'criticism' and they felt under attack (self preservation motive).

2. Define criticism and explain why they were reacting as they were. Then explain how they should, as managers, respond to criticism.

Defining the manager's job

As mentioned above the manager was fulfilling a good deal of the job's requirements effectively but not those segments of the job that involved people. A major part of the manager's role was meeting customers and selling and he was just not doing this. If a manager could not meet this responsibility adequately he or she would have to undertake a different role or leave. Jim therefore:

- Explained his requirements to the branch manager (step one).

- Made sure the branch manager possessed the knowledge and skills to do what Jim was asking (step two).

- Established that the branch manager's attitude was 'willing'. That is, he understood the importance of his selling role and he was prepared to try to meet the revised job requirements (step three).

- Explained he would provide encouragement and monitor and control the branch manager's performance. This would begin to instil self discipline and break old habits (step four and step five).

Following up

Second branch visit - one week later

On Jim's first visit staff seemed to do all in their power to avoid customer contact. Much of this was down to fear of making a mistake, or not knowing an answer to a question. On Jim's second visit this situation had changed. The staff had not become more knowledgeable overnight, but in the temporary appointee they had someone:

- who was willing to help
- to whom a problem could be referred
- who had already run a brief training session with more planned.

Attitudes had already changed.

The branch manager had met his newly defined job requirements with some degree of success. He was prepared to continue as required with a further review in two weeks time. The assistant manager was up to her eyes in paper and loving every minute of it. The supervisor was learning from working closely with the temporary appointee.

Questions:

1. The branch manager has met the job requirements with some success. This proves the manager has the aptitude, which step is this?

2. The assistant manager is up to her eyes in paper and loving every minute, why is she so content?

Answers:

1. Step six

2. The work satisfies her internal motivation, step seven

Third branch visit

The staff
The junior staff were benefiting from experiencing effective performance management:

- They knew what was required of them (step one).
- They were receiving training and coaching to carry out their jobs (step two).
- Their attitudes were far more positive as they began to experience success instead of failure (step three).
- They were being encouraged and supervised effectively (step four).

The management team
The supervisor was learning quickly and the assistant manager continued to meet responsibilities effectively. The branch manager was meeting requirements well but he was not enjoying the role.

Identifying the cause

The manager was now familiar with the 'seven steps' so he and Jim worked through the process:

Step one
The branch manager:

- Understood the requirements of the job.

- Accepted the fact that he had not been meeting the 'people' requirements of the job.

- Recognised that with Jim's help he had started to address these shortcomings by concentrating on his personal sales role.

- Knew if he could master his personal sales responsibilities, Jim would help him master his staff management responsibilities.

There is no point in trying to address all areas requiring improvement at one time.

Step two
Jim had followed up the training received with coaching. This meant the manager did possess the necessary knowledge and skills to carry out the selling role.

Step three
Attitudinally the branch manager accepted meeting the requirements of his job was important. He accepted that what he was being asked to do was part of his job as defined by the organisation.

Step four
The branch manager felt he was being supported and encouraged and the demands were reasonable. He recognised his performance needed to be monitored and controlled. He had found this ensured he kept to his time-plan. Monitoring and control was engendering self discipline.

Step five
He now realised he had habitually avoided doing what was an important aspect of his job.

Step six
The branch manager could meet his personal sales responsibility. He possessed the basic aptitudes. Training and coaching had ensured his knowledge and skill levels produced an entirely acceptable performance in this area.

Step seven
He derived absolutely no satisfaction whatsoever from his personal sales role and did not want to continue. As he and Jim talked about this it became clear to the manager that:

- When he had a 'free hand' he carved out a job that he wanted to do.

- He had never analysed what he was avoiding and why.

- The job he designed for himself satisfied him and he was good at it.

- The customer contact and staff management aspects of the role had never appealed to him.

- He had proven he could meet the customer contact requirements but he just did not enjoy the role.

Solving the problem

Play to strengths not limitations
The manager possessed a lot of strengths and moved to a role that played to those strengths. It was also a role from which he derived a lot of satisfaction. It was a more productive use of his abilities from the organisation's point of view.

Appointing a new manager
The new manager would have to be able to:

- Complete the same 'seven step' exercise with the assistant manager and the supervisor.

- Build on the work of the temporary appointee.

- Possess strengths that complemented those of the assistant manager.

These requirements meant he or she would need to be strong in the 'people' aspects of the manager's role. Jim appointed someone with these strengths.

The assistant manager
The assistant manager was able to develop and met the full job requirements of the role. Though her strengths were still in the administration and control areas, she became an entirely satisfactory sales person and performance manager.

The supervisor
The person brought in on a temporary basis returned to their previous role. The supervisor had learned how to carry out basic supervisory routines.

The staff
The staff developed as individuals and the team spirit was good. The resignations were withdrawn permanently.

The benefits for the organisation

The benefits for the organisation were:

- *Improved business results* - The branch moved up from near the bottom of the league table to the top in twelve months.

- *Better customer service* - The atmosphere in the branch was very welcoming and the staff were confident and competent.

- *Greater efficiency and individual productivity* - The staff developed and did their jobs better.

- *Improved staff morale* - Reduced costs as wastage rates fell.

Conclusion

Jim concluded that:

- A good deal of time and effort is required if a performance manager is to introduce change in an acceptable and beneficial manner.

- Time and effort is also needed to ensure benefits are not lost subsequently.

- Good performance management practice produces results for everybody. The time and effort is worthwhile.

- A 'caring' manager is one that helps people confront issues. The individual as well as the organisation benefits.

Glossary

Attitude. The way we think. Attitudes are based on information, experience or assumption.

Appraisal. An assessment of an individual's performance.

Appraisee. The person whose performance is being assessed.

Appraiser. The person assessing the performance of another.

Appraisal interview. A meeting between the appraiser and appraisee to discuss the assessment.

Best practice. A description of the most efficient or effective way a task can be completed.

Criticism. A reasoned judgement. The judgement is supported by evidence.

Debriefing skills. Interviewing techniques specifically designed to elicit factual information.

Demotivating. Behaviour of a superior that adversely affects the performance of subordinates.

Empathy. Appreciating how others feel in a given situation.

External motivation. What one person does to another engender a desired response.

Habit. An unconscious behaviour.

Internal motivation. The unique mixture of drives and desires each of us possesses.

Job aims. Requirements of a job that lack the precision of a job objective. That is, they lack a standard, a target or a time-scale.

Job inputs. The tasks that need to be completed to achieve a stated output or objective.

Job objectives. Requirements of a job that include a standard or target as a measure and a time-scale.

Job outputs. The required result from the completion of tasks.

On site management. Managing staff who work in the same premises.

Performance management practice. What a performance manager actually does to help someone help him or herself improve or develop performance.

Performance management system. The formalised system and documentation used to set and record job objectives, the outcome of formalised reviews and report on performance.

Personal limitations. The weakest of our abilities despite training and coaching.

Personal strengths. The strongest of our abilities.

Prejudice. An opinion of something or someone that is not based on facts.

Remote site management. Managing staff who are situated in a number of premises that are geographically apart.

Role-play. The demonstration of a skill in a training rather than 'real life' setting.

Self confidence. Recognition of one's relative personal strengths and limitations.

Tasks. An activity that contributes to the achievement of a job objective. It includes a measure (standard or target) and a time-scale.

Task checklist. A listing of important tasks that helps both the job holder and the performance manager manage performance on a day to day basis.

Wastage rate. The percentage rate of turnover in staff numbers.

Index

aptitude-assessing, 77
aptitude-correlation with internal motivation, 86
aptitude-definition, 76
aptitude-examples, 76-78
appraisal-report, 14
appraisees-comments on practice, 15
attitude-box, 39
attitude-definition, 39
attitude-identifying, 40
attitude-managing our own, 42

behaviour-'whats' and 'ways' compared, 21
behaviour-'whats' and 'ways', example, 21
behaviour-'whats' and 'ways', supervision, 22

change-attitude is first step, 109
change-controlling its introduction, 113
change-communicating, 109
change-fundamental, 107
change-initiating, 107
change -that is not fundamental, 108
change-responses to, 107
criticism-definition, 58
criticism-everyday examples and reactions, 59
criticism-giving and receiving, 58, 59
criticism-inviting, 65
criticism-reactions, 60-63

debriefing-everyday example, 100
debriefing-interviews, purpose, 97
debriefing-interviews, structure, 98, 99

debriefing-interviews, style, 99
debriefing-skills, 101
demotivating staff, 67

empathy-develops trust, 23
environment-constituent parts, 45

habit-changing involves criticism, 57
habit-definition, 57
habit-positive and negative, 58
help and hinder questions, 65
help and hinder questions-managing feedback, 66

incentive schemes-compared with recognition, 48

job-inputs, 20, 49, 50
job-objectives, 20
job-outputs, 20
job related training-examples, 32
job requirements-examples, 19

knowledge-assessing, 34
knowledge and skill-relationship, 35

management style, 128
management style-balance, 129
management style-developing, 130
management style-manner, 130
monitoring and control, 49
motivation-external, 45
motivation-external, example, 47
motivation-internal, definition, 45
motivation-internal, exploring, 83
motivation-internal, lack of and job options, 84-86

motivation-the 'carrot approach', 47
motivation-the 'stick approach', 46
motive-fear or self preservation, 35,
36, 42, 46, 59, 66

organisation culture, 131

performance-assessment, the options,
90
performance management -practice, a
contract, 12
performance management-practice
defined, 11
performance management-system,
12-15

self-confidence, 71
self-discipline, 51
skill-assessing, 34, 35
specialist knowledge and skills, 127

staff meetings-assessing quality, 122,
123
staff meetings-controlling, 121
staff meetings-purpose, 116
staff meetings-structure, 116, 117

targets-apportioning, 90, 91
task checklists-constructing, 23
task checklists-example, 23, 24
task checklists-producing, 25, 26
task checklists-using, 20
training-job related, explained, 31
training-best practice, 33
training-coaching, 36
training-job enlargement/enrichment,
34
training-preparatory, 32
training-remedial, 33

vicious circle-example, 68-70

Lightning Source UK Ltd.
Milton Keynes UK
17 August 2010

158544UK00001B/41/P